The House of Loose Screw Heads

Bärbel Kiy

Bärbel Kiy

The House of Loose Screw Heads

or …

Lunatic Castle with a Lakeside View

Bibliographic information published by the Deutsche Nationalbibliothek. The German National Library lists this publication in the German National; detailed bibliographic data are available on the Internet about
http://dnb.dnb.de retrieval bar.

Full paperback edition.
This track was published as an e-book.
Neptunikum Publisher © Bärbel Kiy
Published in Germany 2015
First edition.

Printed in Germany.
Set, cover design, production:
BoD - Books on Demand.
Cover image: © Bärbel Kiy.

ISBN: 978-3-945311-10-3

www.neptunikumverlag.com
10.90 € (D)

Table of Contents

The arrival

or …
The beginning of a journey into the unknown

On the day of her arrival, Angela was to appear in a large hall to be admitted. All of the other new arrivals who had been appointed Tuesday as their arrival day in the polite "invitation" to a multiple week visit at Lunatic Castle with a Lakeside View were to assemble here as well.

Imagine a huge crowd of people on a train platform shortly before the train departs, pushing and shoving, hustling and bustling. The scene here at Lunatic Castle with a Lakeside View in Bad Kleeblatt reminded Angela of the greatest male fantasy figure of our times, Harry Potter, when he found the train platform 9¾ to the secret, magical parallel world at Hogwarts. At least in her eyes, it bore an eerie resemblance to that assembly of non-human, magical creatures who are waiting at King's Cross Station for the Hogwarts Express to the parallel world.

Constant chatter and sizing up: one had to know with whom one would be associating for the next few weeks. One might even be fortunate enough to be cornered and dragged into a conversation.

In the admissions office, in which all new arrivals were processed, things progressed at a snail's pace. Angela had to wait about two and a half hours before she was eventually called in to fill out a questionnaire and be admitted.

During the time she spent waiting in the hall to be admitted, she observed the great tumult around her. Fortunately, her husband Tyler stayed with her and was able to deflect the worst of it from her. The more she observed, the more she had the feeling that she had been consigned to a procession of trash heading toward its final resting place in a comfortable landfill.

It was clear to the casual observer that women were quite capable of doing more than one thing at a time: pushing a suitcase, talking, looking around, sniffing each other, being catty … On the other hand, the men who had arrived here were obviously not capable of multitasking. They could push a suitcase, *or* talk, *or* look around, *or* hit on women *or* scratch their buttocks …

The corrosion of verbal communication will drastically accelerate the stultification of the general populace, she thought as she listened to fragments of the conversation around her. Some examples:

"Did you see the lamp standing back there? The one with the red light bulb. How do you think it glows?"

Answer:

"How do you think it glows? It glows red."

Or: "As if'n we might could really, truly git it good here."

Um … right.

Angela got the distinct impression that the group of people here in Lunatic Castle with a Lakeside View was divided into two categories: fat and stupid. She had been thrown into the same pot here in Bad Kleeblatt with creatures she would never have met in her life, from which she would have intentionally distanced herself.

Plenty of people must have been in the same situation. Being on the same wavelength was the key factor when meeting new people. The vibes Angela was picking up weren't exactly titillating. Her wavelength of rapport had nearly flatlined.

Individual people are quite varied in their composition. This is obvious from outward appearances: fat, thin, tall, short, cute, ugly.

Studly men she was not willing to grace with her courtesy during the first meeting immediately attempted to direct attention to themselves by carrying on loudly with losers in the same game, playing it cool and nonchalant. Saying things like: "Boy howdy, looks like we're going to Disneyworld!"

Or: "Well? You scoped anybody out yet?"

cements their affinity factor during the very first conversation with them. What charmers!

One was led to suspect that these men suffered serious head trauma earlier in their lives and were now brain damaged. In their defense it should be said that they might simply have been sitting in front of the boob tube for far too long. Of course there was no proof for Angela's hypothesis.

Angela's suspicion about the procession of trash only got stronger. Alarm bells went off in her head. On an uneasiness scale of one to ten she was at a full-blown ten and would have preferred to get right back up with her husband, go to the car, and race home. But with her husband's help, she stuck it out.

After she was finally admitted by an employee of the Castle she was permitted to pick up the key to her room from the nurses in the nurses' office. Contrary to the many reservations about a stay in the Castle, the room was quite beautiful. She had been assigned a room in the adjoining hotel, complete with a lakeside view.

The whole thing felt strange, but good.

After the flood of initial impressions, Angela needed to relax some in her room, had to get re-centered, had to let her synapses dangle in the metaphorical wind. After a period of regeneration she could get going again and explore the Castle by herself. But only after she had unpacked her four suitcases into the wardrobe that was mercifully eleven and a half feet long.

At home her husband had asked her while she was packing whether she was planning on including the kitchen sink.

"No, no, I'm just packing a few changes of clothing," had been her answer.

Angela reviewed the day's events in her hotel room. Slowly she calmed down and was able to mentally arrive in the Castle.

On the very same day, Angela was able to discover where she could dine on the comestibles that were distributed daily. Meals were served three and a half times a day. Breakfast, lunch, dinner, and for the famished, who simply couldn't hold out until dinner, there was a snack. Meals were taken in the building across from Angela's temporary lodgings, where the physiotherapy sessions, individual and group therapy, and every other kind of session were also held.

On the second day every one of the uninformed, disoriented new arrivals was assigned to a guide among the residents who had been at Lunatic Castle with a Lakeside View for a while and could show the clueless new arrival around the rooms and acquaint him or her with the customs of the Castle.

These guides discharged this honorable duty more or less willingly and voluntarily. All new boarders were asked upon admittance if they thought they would be up to guiding a new guest around the facility and introducing him or her to life at Lunatic Castle with a Lakeside View in about two weeks time.

The guides were informed of which new, aimless guest they would be initiating on the morning before the tour was to take place. The new patient received a slip of paper with the name and telephone number of their guide printed on it so they could arrange their first meeting together. It was truly a lovely way to be introduced to the buildings and their surroundings.

Angela hoped her guide would be pleasant and likeable, and she was in luck. Her guide was not only quite pleasant, he was also unbelievably likeable. He didn't take himself so seriously – what a nice change of pace!

He was an older, well kempt, slightly portly gentleman, and his name was James. James really threw himself into teaching Angela the ropes around the Castle.

After James had led her through all of the rooms and anterooms in the Castle, he held out his empty hand to her and said:

"Angela, if the tour was to your pleasure, I would be much obliged for a bit of monetary appreciation."

Angela had to smile.

"Gosh, James, I just don't have enough money on me to properly compensate you for your splendid tour."

Both of them started to laugh, and were good friends from that moment on.

James was one the very few people at the Castle who earned Angela's trust during her stay there. Thanks to him, she was quite familiar with the whole of the Castle the next day, and was able to find anything in any of the buildings extremely well.

The grounds were extensive, the paths labyrinthine. The vast premises was incomprehensible for the fresh meat without the proffered help of the guides, who were willing to lead their charges through the solution to the maze, as it were. It was equally challenging for visitors of the ill without the assistance of their resident kin. Without help, it was no trick to get lost.

The new arrivals, gathered in a large reception hall on the day of arrival, were put into groups of "mobile patients" by the sports therapists and had the scheduling rules explained to them.

The day after check-in and every Friday after that the therapy plans were designed. The therapy plan was placed in the resident's room in the evening. Should one decide against one offering or upon another, that was fine – it was the merest trifle to contact the responsible therapist at the designated time and explain one's desires, and the plan was speedily adapted to one's whims. The new plan was once again deposited in the resident's room.

Accommodations were made in the Castle for the general constitution, mobility and immobility of every individual according to the doctor's expert opinion. Every guest's well-being was at the top of the priority list. So far, one felt oneself to be in good hands.

If this wasn't just VIP treatment … but …

Uh-oh. What am I in for? was Angela's first thought as she received her therapy schedule after the sports therapists' peroration.

Questioning her first impression seemed in order after reviewing all of the various and sundry sessions on the plan, for some of the time slots overlapped. In other cases there were exactly five minutes between sessions. Not fun, since in these five minutes one would have to accomplish the feat of finding the right path from one session to the next through the maze of buildings. These requirements could obviously not be met. It was evident that time management and a gift for organization were requisite skills. Angela began having unpleasant premonitions, but in the end things turned out much different than expected.

Hard to believe, but her unpleasant expectations were exceeded in every category. Surely many have heard, read or experienced something about rehabilitation clinics, but compared to what Angela experienced during her stay in Lunatic Castle with a Lakeside View …

Life behind the portcullis

or …
This can't be happening to me

Her worst nightmares paled in comparison, many a day it seemed surreal, and at all times it resembled a poorly researched book. Oh, well. The best stories come from real life, she told herself.

People swarmed from all sides, from right and left, from behind and from in front, to meals, the various sessions, and therapy like alien hive drones, all thinking seemingly being done by a central instance that broadcast instructions over the airwaves. This is either the weirdest terrestrial sight I've ever seen or conclusive proof that aliens really do live amongst us, thought Angela.

She was also fascinated by the various dialects she overheard.

"You talkin' 'bout upper B'varia, you talkin' 'bout thuh durn purtiest parts uh thuh country," came from one corner.

From other places one could hear.

"You do a little ze talking, you do a little ze listening."

"I double pahkt my cah out front.", and "Man, dat wuz some lot uh snow!"

Man, oh man. There was just nothing else like it. Surely all sixteen German states were represented in this "game without borders". The question remained whether the Castle employed translators for all of the dialects, Angela mused on her way to the cafeteria.

There were only two cafeterias for all one hundred seventy people, but a dietician gave every new patient an assigned seat in one of the two locations for the duration of his or her stay on the first day.

Angela thought to herself: Jackpot! They've got everything here! Could I be so lucky? Might they possibly have a professional chef?

Unfortunately, Angela discovered during her stay that there were certainly no professional chefs engaged in the kitchen. More probably they were cafeteria cooks, or perhaps army cooks … or even assistants to army cooks.

Angela presumed she was lucky: she had been given a seat at a large table in the larger of the two cafeterias at which to take her meals. The larger cafeteria encompassed two buffets, the smaller cafeteria only one. It was a fallacy on her part to assume because of this that food was bountifully available. If one was not waiting at the entrance to the cafeteria at precisely the prescribed time, tough luck: one had to make due with the divots left by those who came first. Sometimes mere minutes after the cafeteria opened there was hardly anything left to eat. The buffets had been decimated. Here, there were only the quick and the hungry. It was also a big mistake to imagine that empty trays, salad bowls or other implements of food containment would be refilled. Once empty, always empty.

To avoid a backup, the patients were divided across two timeslots for meals. Angela was told on her first day in residence which of the two timeslots she had been assigned to. But there was a catch. Seats were assigned once to each group. Should one wish to deviate from the prescribed mealtime, because one was hungry earlier for instance, one was simply out of luck. The seat was occupied by another patient. The only ways to nourish oneself ahead of schedule would have been to share a seat or to sit on someone's lap.

It was a nice touch that there was a green adhesive strip at every place indicating which patient was to sit there, and how long they were staying, much like place cards. These remained on the table for the duration of one's stay, and were not to be removed. It left the impression that the patients were not trusted to remember which seat at which table was theirs, and how long they were to be in residence.

Angela completely agreed with the implicit message: we're all not as smart as we look. After all, I know I'm no rocket scientist, she thought.

Days were planned from reveille to retreat, so to speak. This was good for some patients who needed clear, strict instructions, but it had its dark side. The tyranny of the schedule was omnipresent. Weekdays from Monday through Friday were cast in a rigid, constant thirty-minute tempo, so the afflicted had scant opportunity to engage in activities of their own volition until after the end of the working day, typically around four in the afternoon.

"Gosh, they really don't leave us much private time. I suppose they plan it this way so we don't get any stupid ideas. Heaven only knows what could happen then!"

This from Molly, one of Angela's classmates in her abs, legs, and buns class, which she had gleefully wheedled out of the sports therapist upon encountering him in a long corridor on the mad dash between therapy rooms on the first day of class selection.

To forestall the eventuality that Angela might forget when, in which building, and in which room every one of her appointments was, there was always the daily schedule. Everything – really everything – was listed in the daily schedule. Heaven forbid anyone should have to employ his or her brain! Even all three meals were printed with their allotted time slots, just as sessions and therapy of all kinds were printed with time and precise location.

Patients here were always on the move. Ack! thought Angela as she stepped out of the shower, looked at the clock, and realized she was late once again. The quiet time she had been pining for was a no-show here at the Castle. Rest and relaxation were not to be had. She was more stressed here than at home. The only plus as far as she was concerned was that meals were served and a maid cleaned the room.

Weekends were her own, so she was determined to free herself from the system, from the diktat.

Thus far, she had been under the impression that patients were in places like the Castle and other similarly worthy institutions to counteract stress, hecticness, and the pressures of a schedule, but it was obviously not the intention, the highest goal, of the therapists and doctors in the Castle to let their patients unwind.

It must be said about this system that patients were told everything on their schedules was an offering that could be freely partaken of. If Angela couldn't or didn't want to attend one of the sessions, no problem, she had only to tell one of the nurses on duty. That was the theory, anyway. In practice she almost never saw this. Few took advantage of this offer of abstinence.

Most were reluctant to because they had received purple folded cards at the beginning of their stay as proof of their visits to therapy sessions. The therapists signed these cards every time the patients visited their assigned therapy sessions. This proof of active involvement was sent with a concluding letter and the rehabilitation clinic's evaluation of the patient to the health insurer.

The hidden agenda that Angela intuited behind this procedure was that the patients quickly reenter the working world. They shouldn't get too comfortable where they were. Was it better to feel like they were truly back at work, being rushed from one meeting to the next? Why should the burnout patients or the clinically depressed be allowed to rejuvenate? Why? It was simply too much to ask that the patients be allowed to conquer their problems. The only "advantage" Angela could discern was that some of the afflicted were given structure and guided through the day by this form of organization. Ignoring this point for a moment, it was plain that those who would otherwise have been in offices should not be permitted to fall out of synch with the rhythm of the working world.

Angela had arrived in her hotel room whipped from cardiovascular training, and now lay in bed exhausted from fighting through her strenuous day, reflecting.

I guess I'll have to relax at home after rehab so I can process the many extraordinary moments and de-stress. That was her plan, but she had just started getting acclimated to the Castle, and still had a long way to go here.

After speaking with many of the other patients, Angela discovered that many of them felt the same way. Many were stressed and were looking forward to going home.

There were a few, however, abandoned and abandoning all, who never wanted to go home, who would have loved to continue living a protected life behind the "portcullis", as it were, here in the Castle.

Life writes the best stories

or …
What soap opera did I land in?

The amount of testosterone here at Lunatic Castle with a Lakeside View was almost palpable.

Men who would have been third rate at best in the outside world beyond the portcullis, who would have been fodder for casting shows or reality television of the worst sort, deluded themselves into believing they could hook up with an alpha female here in the Castle. But it didn't stop there. Mating was obviously the primary goal. These men were in heat in the worst way.

And how exactly did the chosen, the selected, the adored react?

Hard to believe, but these grown-up women giggled and gloried in the attention. Women upwards of fifty suddenly fancied themselves adolescents again and responded to advances with all of the allure they could still muster. The lights were still on in some of the uteruses present. It's a sure bet some of them were thinking, "Before my biological clock completely stops ticking …"

Some of the women even dyed streaks into their hair to be more visible from low Earth orbit, but a pig wearing lipstick is still a pig.

Without a doubt some of them imagined they were letting a racing boat into bed with them, but alas, it was instead the Titanic.

From time to time it was too much for Angela, and she wanted to scream, to shake these women back to their senses and return them from their fantasies to the reality of their own world in the here and now. Unfortunately, Cupid seemed to have arrived before her at the lakeside Castle and had emptied his quiver.

Since she remained impervious to these testosterone bombs, she was lucid enough to arrive at her own conclusion: she was witnessing occasional localized cases of dementia. One was often led to wonder what parallel universe the demented had to think they were in for their fantasies to be manifested.

Some of the aforementioned men were finally able to find women at Lunatic Castle with a Lakeside View they could touch without having to inflate them first. To be fair, there were surely some among these men who still had active, consensual sex – when their partners fell asleep with their mouths open.

Harking to the call of hormones, bones were being jumped left and right. Test drilling was commonplace. After all, sooner or later partnerless sex yields no more surprises. Even genetic condition was increasingly ignored. Bunga, bunga.

Perhaps Angela should explain to these women in small, understandable words that German men only remained aroused for eleven seconds. After eleven seconds without the answering warmth of a female body, his erection collapses like a soufflé removed from the oven too soon.

Many a testosterone bomb was dropped on a menstrual minefield here.

Quite a few patients here suffered from a thrombosis of the emotional artery, and many men were looking for a new plaything behind their partners' backs.

There were a few well-travelled residents in the lakeside Castle who followed the example of the city of Esperantina. In this city not far from Rio de Janeiro the Day of the Orgasm has been celebrated every year since May 9th, 2002. The citizens of this city view the orgasm as a gift from God. These world travellers, who had declared themselves missionaries of this creed, joyfully celebrated this queer holiday, selflessly offering their own worldly flesh for the festivities, but naturally only to win new converts to their cause. In that sense, all those mentioned here enjoyed a good holiday every day.

Angela ruminated on the drama being acted out before her eyes. It has been scientifically proven that human genes are ninety-eight percent the same as pig genes. Only two percent of their genes result in men not growing a curly tail. That, however, is no excuse for trying to get as many of the female patients as possible in a clinic for psychosomatic sickness to gently stroke their throbbing love warrior out of his hiding place.

Maybe the way to infuse these women with more objectivity was through agitation. Perhaps investing in a bull horn and leaflets and inciting a riot would get these women to remove their rose-colored glasses.

Where's a rabid feminist when you needed one? Where are her followers? Was this territory declared a feminist-free zone while I wasn't watching? Girls, I need you!

Hellooo!

Am I the only one fighting on this front? thought Angela.

Many of the men present wanted a double garage, so to speak, in their relationships. At home they presumably had a well maintained, classic automobile, perhaps from the same year they were born, and here at the Castle they were in the market for a brand-new hybrid that didn't have many miles on the odometer, and hadn't really been broken in yet, or, even better, hadn't been broken in at all. The new owner wanted to break this lovely new model in himself.

It's superfluous to state that permanent, committed companionship was exotic here. Here, men and women alike considered the constancy of relationships a charade. This begged the question what their wives, husbands, or partners thought of this view.

Quarrels, arguments, rows with an inclination to violence were a foregone conclusion. Married, filing separately.

Here in the harbor from the storm many marriages must surely have wrecked on the rocks within sight of the shore.

Testosterone surplus

or …
Randy tomcats

In the hotel in which Angela was quartered there were two elevators. One of them was always out of order …

The elevators must have predated Noah's ark. Every time it took a few full minutes for them to arrive on the required floor. Angela considered it a kind of torture to have to wait for the appearance of the elevator every time.

The time stuck in the elevator as well as the time stuck waiting on the elevator were ripe times to be approached by one of the testosterone bombs. They seized the opportunity during the long wait to make shameless overtures. Most of the men at the clinic were obviously being led solely by their animal instincts. Ninety percent of them must have been listening to the devil seated on their left shoulder whispering incessantly "mate, mate, mate!"

Angela had just gotten in the elevator with another patient she recognized when he asked in a circuitous fashion, "Say, why is it so hard to find the right partner?"

Angela countered with a question of her own: "Why do you ask? Is the wrong woman sitting at home waiting for you?"

Either the man hadn't heard her, or he slyly overheard her question, for he pressed on with his trash talk.

"The table is set and there's quite a spread on it, if you know what I mean, but still I can't find a woman to sit down and enjoy the meal", the degenerate continued to insinuate. Angela didn't reply. Instead, she simply gave him a questioning look and got off the elevator without wasting her breath on him. What a great way to start the day!

What does trash do as it ages? It becomes more full of life, thought Angela as she looked for Molly in the yard in front of the Castle.

The female guests at Lunatic Castle with a Lakeside View were ogled every morning by the testosterone bombs staying in the hotel. As soon as everyone got in the elevator the Schwarzenegger wannabes, who in fact looked more like Marlon Brando in his later years, made their moves and it was decided which of the females had passed the test and would be briefly permitted to play the role of eye candy on the arm of one of the men, or more importantly, playmate in his bed.

What in the world must the men here have thought of themselves? With respect to their hormone profile they were all demonstrably men, but not one of the male patients here met Angela's most basic definition of a man in any other way.

Typical come-ons from these paragons of masculinity during the elevator ride ran from "What's on your plan for today?" to:

"If you're not doing anything special, how about we go grab a cup of coffee together?"

Or: "You want to go into the city with me?"

The pinnacle was:

"You're here, too?" Naturally these questions were only asked of those women they thought to be receptive to their blunt advances.

Angela was asked this last question point blank on one occasion while she was waiting on the elevator with Molly and some other women.

"Just a moment. I'll ask my friend," replied Angela, and turned to her right where Molly was standing.

"Molly, am I here, too?"

"Yes," smiled Molly. Angela turned back to the testosterone bomb and retorted snippily

"It seems I am here, too, yes."

Just as Angela decided things couldn't get stupider, she received a lesson from the bottom of the abyss of stupidity. About two hours after the aforementioned confrontation Angela was in the elevator when she was asked another of these brilliant questions:

"Would you like to talk about your problems with me?"

"Sure. I can't imagine pouring my heart out to someone better than you," she answered with more than a little edge in her voice.

I'm sure you're only available as a double pack, you old goat: you and your huge ego shooter, she thought during the remainder of the elevator ride to the ground floor.

It was irritating. Lamentations flew left and right here at the lakeside Castle. Would have, could have, should have, and if only.

Many of these male pussycats rubbed, batted, and purred like fat, old, randy tomcats to reach their goal. Their fur was nearly rubbed off, their claws dull from playful scratching, and their paws bore the scars of their many failed attempts, but these tomcats were indomitable in their mating efforts.

During her stay she even heard this unbelievable sentence:

"I can make a woman very, very happy."

Angela looked at the two people talking standing at the entrance, or exit, depending on how you took it. She was walking past the smokers into one of the buildings on her way to group therapy. God's gift to women must have been pushing sixty, and the woman he was talking to can't have been thirty, by the looks of it.

She entered the building and thought: The question is, how could the good man make a woman nearly thirty years his junior so happy? The only way I can think of is if he closed her bedroom door – from the outside.

She often heard this one: "I understand women. If one of the other patients causes you a problem, or if you have anything else on your mind and just need to get a load off your chest, I always have an open ear for you."

Did the man really mean an open ear, or perhaps an open zipper, always ready.

Angela hoped that this chitchat coming from an unemployable man was nothing more than a phrase repeated without meaning. He couldn't really mean that silly platitude, could he? He must have been dreaming. But how nice of this man who so understood women to gallantly, touchingly be so concerned for the well-being of the female patients, and so guilelessly and selflessly.

Why didn't these men ever get tired of hearing their own voices?

It made Angela shudder that all of the even halfway attractive women at the Castle constantly had to fend off the advances of multitudinous, well, let's just call it like it is, sex-starved men. What a hassle.

Most days Angela felt quite put upon by the male inmates' pushy behavior, even if she wasn't directly involved. These extreme behavioral patterns are probably a direct result of the fact that large portions of a snail's genes remain in human DNA, and in the final analysis men on the make can't do much about their sliminess. The poor things, thought Angela after one of her morning elevator trips through the gauntlet.

She had heard everything. Really, everything.

How about this one: "If I happen to be in your town, maybe we could grab a bite to eat together."

Or this: "We could go out together somewhere, if you'd like." "Give me your e-mail address so we can trade information and pictures," when Angela was sure there were no pictures to trade.

"How about we trade telephone numbers?" *Sure,* thought Angela, *why not give him your cell phone number so you can be available for him day and night.*

Angela discovered the sad result of removing herself from the line of fire of the men and their constant come-ons, of turning down invitation after invitation and making it clear that she was not interested in the testosterone bombs: she was considered arrogant and aloof.

"You think you're better than everyone else, don't you?" One man threw in her face after she had rejected his invitation to the movies. It was, of course, only the petty man's injured pride.

Life's neither a circus, nor a walk in the park, my dear radiation poisoned men, thought Angela after the aforementioned suitor had loudly aired his opinion through a stuffed-up nose.

What tempting offers from all sides! Sometimes, after so much masculine tender loving care, so much unwanted attention, she could almost feel her gag reflex. Nonetheless, she had to admit that the evidently debilitated man's accusation was correct. Here in the Castle there were only four decent conversationalists from whom Angela could choose: Molly, Thomas, Ina, and David.

Exercise is good for you

or …
He who exercises willingly gets what he deserves

All of those disinclined from exercise out there, be forewarned: no one in the Castle escaped exercise. Exercise releases large quantities of endorphins into the bloodstream, as everyone knows, and these endorphins were supposed to dissolve the logjam of depression that had built up.

Excepting Angela, no one seemed truly to believe that exercise was a positive experience. She never noticed anyone else taking advantage of extra chances for exercise as she happily did, or following her lead and negotiating with the sports therapists for more opportunities to exercise.

Most of the other participants invented excuses to get out of sports or trimmed the already insufficient thirty minutes by some twenty minutes. Had no one educated them that exercise has a positive effect on mood, physical constitution, and, last but not least, one's figure?

No, it was even better: Angela got the impression that they were doing everything in their power to avoid losing a single ounce.

Those present who harbored an aversion to physical fitness drank lots of soda and fruit juice, liked plenty of cream and sugar in their coffee, and ate chips, cheese curls, fast food, candy and other sweets, but heaven forbid anything fat free or healthy. Healthy food like vegetables and fruit or even lite drinks like Coke Lite or seltzer water cause headaches, heartburn, hives, or some similar malady. One of the other patients actually said this to Angela.

Many of the patients were clearly suffering from a newly discovered condition: Alzheimer's bulimia. In this condition one eats unhealthy, calorie rich food the whole day, but forgets to barf it up again at night.

The natural consequence was, of course, that they maintained their current level of obesity or started tipping the scales much farther. Their Body Mass Index (BMI) could hardly be calculated anymore.

Beyond all this, they had missed the point of exercise. The mantra is "fit through exercise," not "fat from no exercise." These patients were simply the result of their genetic predispositions and their overeating, and there was no changing that!

Such a pity, for it could only be through a new insight like healthy eating, sports or more movement in general, perhaps walking or taking the stairs instead of the elevator, that the many Michelin men here, the fat, farting wombats (if the reader will excuse the comparison), as well as the corpulent women reminiscent of Ruben's models and the portly men with flab hanging everywhere on their bodies and figures like a pill could hope to move without difficulty again, without breaking a sweat after the second or third step and wheezing like a stranded walrus.

Then there were those who had had a liposuction years before and were still waiting for the flabby skin left behind to disappear. All of these dear patients could return to an active life if they so chose.

It was a safe bet that these patients' favorite piece of furniture was the refrigerator, as long as it was always full. Angela 1 thought, They must have a picture of their favorite home furnishing, full to overflowing, always close at hand in their wallets to carry them through the hungry times when all they have is the picture and the memory of food to satiate themselves.

It also seemed highly likely that these patients never dined where food was served á la carte, but rather took advantage of all-you-can-eat buffets and XXL eateries. The poor things would surely have had to spend most of a paycheck in an á la carte restaurant to quell their burning hunger and leave the restaurant glutted.

There were many here who engaged in sports without having to move. Angela had heard other patients say: "Sports? Sure, I watch 'em!"

Or: "I play chess. That's a kind of sport."

This was no surprise, for these residents moved like a horse on roller skates.

While she was still at home she had looked forward to using the fitness studio in the rehabilitation clinic. She had gleaned all the information on it the Internet had to offer and had even studied all of the individual exercises and the order of their execution. Her disappointment was thus all the greater when she discovered from some of the other patients that joining the fitness club while checked in to the Castle was an almost impossible undertaking.

"Go ahead and try your luck," said Thomas.

"I've heard that a few people before you tried and failed, but maybe they'll let you work out there since you're staying in the hotel. Good luck!" "Nothing ventured, nothing gained," responded Angela and headed for the fitness studio.

Her curiosity had been aroused. She was determined to find out for herself if the rumors floating around Lunatic Castle with a Lakeside View had a grain of truth to them.

It was already her fifth day in the Castle, so she walked over to the adjoining fitness club. It was located on the second floor of a building neighboring the Castle. The vista of Bad Kleeblatt out the panorama windows in the fitness studio was beautiful.

Angela gazed upon the lovely landscape around the lake, bemused. When she arrived on the second floor where the fitness studio was, she was greeted at the reception desk by a nice young woman.

"How may I assist you?" she asked kindly.

"I would like to work out in your club for the next thirty days, if possible," Angela replied. Smiling, the nice young woman answered,

"Quite possible. We'd love to have you. Payment is one hundred euros cash in advance."

That's not bad, thought Angela, and reached for her wallet. The nice young woman, still smiling, continued … "But you're a guest at the hotel, not a patient, right?"

She didn't understand the purpose of this question, and her baffled brain suddenly abandoned her, leaving her to answer, "I've been admitted as a patient of Lunatic Castle and am staying in the hotel located next to it, but I would still like to work out on your machines, visit classes, and otherwise take advantage of what your club has to offer every day."

The smile froze on the nice young woman's face, and she responded: "I'm afraid we don't offer membership to patients of the Castle. We've had unfortunate incidents here in the past with patients from Lunatic Castle. I'm sorry to have to say that I have to reject your application for a thirty day membership."

Angela was crushed. This was obviously just an excuse.

This was nothing more than an attempt to justify the decision not to let patients of the Castle work out here. Obviously they were being discriminated against – with a smile, no less.

She was shocked and asked the nice young woman: "Whom else can I have a word about this with in this club? I don't understand your reason, and I would like a clear an competent answer."

The nice young woman replied, "There's no one here responsible for signing up new club members except me, but if my answer doesn't suit you, you are always free to speak to the head physician at the clinic."

Good tip, thought Angela. She turned on her heels and exited through the large glass door toward the elevator feeling cheated. On the way, she passed two men going the other way. The first one was the bodyguard type. One could see in him the roots of human evolution. The way he held his body and walked was more than reminiscent of a primate or, at best, a Neanderthal. A fossil, he was obviously a genetic relict left by the wayside along the path of Man's ascension. Any paleoanthropologist would have been delighted to get his hands on this specimen.

The second man looked like he had just been flown in from Japan – he looked for all the world like a sumo wrestler.

So the two of you are welcome guests in this renowned club, are you? You're permitted to work out here? thought Angela as she stomped furiously into the waiting elevator.

If only, when asked if I was a patient or only staying in the hotel, instead of admitting that I was a patient, I had simply answered, "Yes, I'm just staying in the hotel!"

Angela cursed herself.

But lies catch up with you quickly.

The owners of the fitness club appeared to believe that the patients, no, the *guests* of the Castle suffered from mental retardation.

A short time later Angela l stood on the head physician's floor, ready to spit fire. She felt discriminated against by the employees of the fitness club. Her behavior on this lofty floor was befitting to the incident.

Have I degenerated into a second-class citizen?

Who am I, anyway?

Why did the employees of the fitness studio discredit me?

Have I gone wacko just because I checked into the Castle?

She continued to feed baleful thoughts of this ilk to the squall ripping through her mind.

Angela was prepared to give the head physician a piece of her mind about being denied temporary membership in the fitness studio. She marched right past the dour anteroom dragon and made a beeline for the head physician's office. Regretably, the dour anteroom dragon was faster and put an abrupt halt to Angela's rage-fuelled march.

"You can't just waltz in here and barge into the head physician's office," commanded the dragon. Just watch me, lady, thought Angela, but exercising restraint she acquiesced.

"Fine. I'll just have to sit here waiting (there was a row of chic chairs in the anteroom) until he can see me."

"That could be a while", responded the dour anteroom dragon.

"I've lived through worse," said Angela, and remained firmly glued to her chair.

About ten minutes later she was allowed into the head physician's office, and was greeted at the door by the head physician himself. Upon entering the office she took a seat in a stylish armchair. She looked around. The office was tastefully decorated, and was quite to Angela's liking.

She got right to the point and hotly informed him of her visit to the adjacent fitness studio and all that had transpired there, then demanded to know what his position was on what the employee in the studio had told her.

Despite his attempts to attenuate the effects of the employee's ill tidings, he was compelled to confirm the decision.

"Unfortunately, for insurance reasons it is not possible for patients of the Castle to join the nearby fitness studio. My hands are tied. I can't make an exception for you. Allow me to remind you that we have adequate fitness course offerings here on our own grounds."

If only he would tell me what offerings among the currently available courses he considers adequate, thought Angela.

It had become clear to her that she would not be able to effect any changes at this time and in this place, so she left the room depressed. The physician is one to talk, she thought. He can't feel the veritable life preservers growing on his hips. She was left no alternative but to settle for the fitness courses offered by the Castle, even if they did seem to be nothing more than the bare minimum.

It would obviously be a more meaningful use of Angela's time to wait for Godot than to try fighting her way into the fitness club.

The “outbreak” of illness

or …
I love you, you love me, we’re a happy family

Angela, as already mentioned, wasn’t gung ho about, or rather was truly disinclined from submitting to her assigned plan on Saturdays and Sundays. Of course there were no therapy sessions, but the weekend began nonetheless at 8:15 a.m. with breakfast and ended at 6:45 p.m. with dinner.

So she withdrew from the tyrannical schedule on the weekends and did not appear for breakfast or any of the other planned meals. This promptly precipitated a call to her room from the lady at the reception desk on her second weekend at the Castle.

“The folks sitting around you at the table are worried about you,” cooed the pleasant, female voice on the other end of the telephone.

“Has anything happened?”, inquired the pleasant telephone voice.

“The ladies and gentlemen standing here in front of me at the reception desk want to know if everything is okay. Are you all right? You haven’t come to eat today at all.”

“Thanks for your concern, but I’m fine”, Angela answered the friendly telephone voice.

“I just want some time to myself, that’s all. Thanks for asking.”

She was immediately suspicious. It just so happened that a new virus had been spreading through Lunatic Castle with a Lakeside View in the last few days.

The clinic administration had been posting and handing out flyers about the virus. They had been distributing disinfectant to sanitize "contaminated hands". The bottles were placed all through the public areas of the Castle, and one could generously slather it on oneself on the clinic's dime.

Consequently, Angela immediately suspected that her new best buddies at the cafeteria table were more concerned for themselves than for her, but the situation was, of course, carefully presented to mean something else, namely that here at the Castle everyone watched out for everyone else, that everyone had your back. Naturally, this was purely selfless. Sure. And if you believe that …

Plainly an alarming number of the patients had been contaminated with the virus. That's why there have been so many empty chairs in both cafeterias recently, she ruminated.

It should be noted that Angela had never received so much attention from the people at her cafeteria table as on this weekend.

After the fiasco with her tablemates and the call from the receptionist, she made sure to call ahead of time and inform the powers that be when she was not intending on eating in the cafeteria, though it riled her to have other people's expectations imposed upon her.

If so many people behind the portcullis were contaminated with the virus, why was it that the clinic administration kept admitting new patients? Tuesday through Thursday new patients kept rolling in.

Since she had only asked herself this question, she answered it for herself as well. Who else could have? Long live vile Mammon! *Pecunia non olet.*

The large, expensive Castle had to be kept running .

The weekend

or …
Finally amongst "normal" people

Angela always looked forward to the weekend.

As previously explained, she never went to the Castle to eat on the weekends.

On Saturdays during her stay of many weeks, she treated herself to a large breakfast with free coffee refills at the nearby village café and read the local newspaper.

She usually loitered blissfully a good ninety minutes in the village café. No one got on her nerves here. She could eat in peace and quiet.

Her husband Tyler "flew" in regularly every Saturday afternoon. It was then she could rejoin the pulse of the real world, laugh, lead "normal" conversations, sense the red blood coursing through her veins, and feel good.

He drove her to the nearest big city.

They went walking together, did some window shopping, bought clothes – all the things most women love to do. Her husband always was and remains a superb fashion consultant. He has taste, patience, and an excellent sense of humor.

Her weight loss clearly provoked his pity.

Every week Tyler took her to a classy steak house in the best part of the city where she was to gormandize to her heart's content.

Angela managed to consume two steaks at about three quarters of a pound each and a salad from the salad bar during these evenings out. And she could return to the salad bar as often as she liked.

It was not a seldom occurrence that men and women sitting at tables near hers in the steakhouse on these Saturday evenings were aghast at the quantity of food she was able to put away. If you've got it, you've got it, she thought as she noticed the astonished gazes.

The thought of home gave Angela's beleaguered soul a dose of wellness!

On Sundays she skipped breakfast. She relaxed until midday, and as a result didn't rise until 11 a.m. She did some morning gymnastics, checked her e-mail, and surfed the Internet for a while. Angela checked in to her online community and kept up with what people were doing, then set off into the village around 2 p.m.

Sometimes she was able to see the last remnants of activity on these sleepy Sundays in Bad Kleeblatt, and she could go to the café she had grown fond of and have a big piece of pie with lots of whipped cream.

A cup of aromatic coffee rounded out the experience. The coffee in the café tasted extraordinarily good.

When she returned to her hotel room from these outings, she took time to pursue her hobbies. She would read or otherwise occupy herself, then eat some sushi and drink a glass of red wine as her day faded to its conclusion.

Oh, how delectable the forbidden fruit does taste, she thought all the while during her epicurean pampering every Sunday.

Every weekend brought her closer to home, be it fraught with its own problems as it may.

But in the face of all of the accumulated problems here and the pushiness from the hardcore lesbians, eccentric gays, transsexuals, sex-addicted women and men, and the men in heat at Lunatic Castle with a Lakeside View, she could hardly wait to get home. Her mental reconnection with home every weekend and the expectation of returning there soon lifted her spirits beyond all measure.

Saturday, again and again …

or …
How not to act your age

The weekend was burningly pined for starting at the very beginning of the new week, because the weekend promised the highlight of the whole week for many patients: a trip to the adjacent disco and its large reserve of that otherwise taboo substance, alcohol.

Anyone found in the rehab clinic with alcohol or in bed with the opposite sex, or presumably the same sex as well, was summarily sent packing. While this may have sounded tempting to some patients, it carried a heavy penalty. Those caught in the act had to carry the full cost of their stay at the clinic themselves. Should one be on the receiving end of such an involuntary dismissal, the resulting bill was no joke. Angela had heard that an average stay here ranged in cost from some twelve to fourteen thousand euros. This was probably enough money to convince most anyone to curb their passions, to still the throbbing urges in their loins.

In the disco next to the clinic the alpha female could drink until the gamma male finally appealed to her. Under the influence one was quick to say yes to anything erotic, the idols of lust and sensuality reveled in their followers' worship, and suddenly there were plenty of visions of beauty to feast one's eyes upon.

The impassioned playthings smiled winsomely as if they were a winning lottery ticket. Some of the men's pituitary glands were thanking them for coming to the disco, and their hypothalamuses had to move like an Olympian to direct the rapid buildup of hormones to the correct compartments.

In the time the aforementioned females had spent primping in the bathroom, entire galaxies had risen and fallen. They put on their faces with such devotion that, dolled up as they were, they left the impression they were on their way to the Bambi or Oscar awards ceremony.

Those wild about dancing were on the dance floor, while those who could hold their drink were congregated at the bar. The dance floor, however, was perhaps one hundred twenty square feet. It was so cozy that the chemistry could get intense on the very first dance!

The gamma males didn't need the makeshift beauty salon treatment in their hotel rooms like the women did, of course. Even a splash of CK One or similar cologne, so common in the outside world, was a rarity here.

All present, especially the men indicated, were convinced that the pheromone androstenone secreted with their own sweat was sufficient olfactory enhancement that spreading their own natural aphrodisiac was attractant enough – and they were right. It worked like a charm. Quite obviously these men who had no need for commercial scents were able to obnubilate the women's remaining functional senses with their masculine body odor. In this manner some seventy percent of them achieved the effect they desired and reached their goal.

Who could have imagined it … the women here turned their brains off one after the other. Estrogen oozed out of their pores, their sexual desire rose beyond measure, and their nether regions screamed: take us now!

It was entertaining to watch how some of the pairs forming became certifiable idiots after ingesting high proof liquids. These couples demonstrated great deficits in their motor skills and, judging by their behavior, in their mental processes.

It was noticeable that the chosen partner's face faded from memory in the time it took to use the toilet, so the seeker was left to belt out a mating call to the sought. It was not seldom that someone standing on the outside watching this was forced to ask herself: "What good is a name if you can't remember the face that goes with it?"

Watching and listening to all of this was fun for the uninitiated and the sober.

The beta and gamma men hit on anything female and sometimes male that wasn't able to climb a tree by the count of three. Those who were able to climb were still pursued. The last one and a half to two million years of human evolution had plainly left their mark on these men.

The men had one million sperm available to them every day, but the women only had one egg a month, so the men could spray around their abundant chromosomes with abandon. It didn't matter what they screwed as long as it was female, or maybe male – in other words, a warm body. Generally speaking, fidelity was archaic here, out of style, a relic of days of yore. Humans were not made for monogamy. When the men felt that itch in their gonads, there was no holding them back.

Some present suffered from diminished visual perception. One in every three images of the twelve per second necessary for the human brain to perceive the world as a continuous whole was filtered out under the powerful influence of various alcoholic beverages.

Fragments of conversation didn't want to connect on their own, since life's soundtrack was equivalently compressed.

Alcohol consumption, hazy visuals, and the loss of one's own native language required great concentration to do anything.

Writers for soap operas must get their ideas from scenes such as these.

Pairings that would have been impossible in real life happened here and lasted perhaps the length of their stay.

The one time Angela allowed herself to be bulldozed into going to the disco on a Saturday night, she was immediately sized up by one of the men from the bottom of the barrel and assaulted with the come-on:

"This joint's really jumping, eh?"

"Yes," retorted Angela, "but if you would leave, it would be that much emptier."

"Man, it's loud here," shouted another horny man in Angela's ear.

"If you would refrain from bellowing at me, it wouldn't be so loud," was her reply.

As soon as she had seated herself at a table with her girlfriends and ordered a glass of wine, the next beta or gamma specimen sidled up to her table – exactly how poor his ranking was in the pack was difficult to determine in the dim light. He nonchalantly asked her: "Do you mind if I smoke?"

"No, not at all," conceded Angela, "in fact, I don't even mind if you flat out burn."

Might be good for roasting marshmallows, she thought.

Contact was made and dates at the disco were arranged differently depending on the personal habits and preferences of those involved. Non-smokers typically made arrangements on the elevator (where else?). Those of an intellectual bent, those who had some culture, people who liked to participate in discussion groups and spoke proper German hooked up in reading rooms, during film evenings or during one of the scheduled evening entertainments. The militant smokers connected with each other in their smoking groups or in one of the delineated smoking areas.

Angela was on the receiving end of one such invitation to a date: "Say, you wanna go to the disco with me tonight? We can dance a little, drink a little, and decide where it goes from there later," proposed the cocksure contestant in this one-sided competition.

How could this fail to excite? She thought concerning this crass attempt at seduction. Even if I were dead I wouldn't let you touch me. I would rather blow strawberry flavored cotton candy out of my rear than get involved with you, she thought with a shudder. Imagine her admirer's surprise when she turned down his well-meaning, generous invitation with the endearing words.

"No thanks, I don't want to go to the disco with you, and I will most certainly be sleeping alone in my bed tonight."

He was instantly deflated. How could she turn him down? Reject him? He had done nothing more than nobly offer himself to an aging dame to sweeten her lonely evening.

Who did she think she was?

After repelling his advance he gave her the silent treatment for a substantial portion of her remaining stay. This was undoubtedly meant to teach her a lesson and to make her amenable to later dates, possible rendezvous. How could she not throw herself at the feet of such a man? How could she spurn his invitation?

She was free of his base comments and cheap come-ons for a while. Angela felt herself in this sense extraordinarily lucky. After this encounter she felt absolutely confirmed in her prejudices concerning the meat market here at the rehabilitation clinic.

As previously noted, eighty percent of the testosterone bombs were successful in spreading their seeds at Lunatic Castle with a Lakeside View. Hard to believe, but true.

Those at the Castle had swung their doors wide to mental decay and the deterioration of decorum.

Beginning and advanced sports

or …
Introducing the watt groups

Angela noticed again and again that much value was placed on sports at Lunatic Castle with a Lakeside View.

The sports groups were arranged around the number of watts generated while exercising. There were the twenty-five watt groups, the fifty watt groups, and the seventy-five watt groups.

Man, oh man, talk about a powerhouse:

Those in the seventy-five watt groups were the best, the studliest. All of them tried to outdo the others. It didn't matter what the sport was, it didn't matter whether man or woman, every one of them wanted to be the best. They gave their all every time.

The fifty watt groups were more laid back. The competition for the best physical performance wasn't quite as out of hand.

Things were naturally downright relaxed in the twenty-five watt groups, and the average age of the group members was much higher. This is where the generation over seventy was placed. These groups were a microcosm of the aging demographic in Germany. The twenty-five watt groups felt like they were nothing more than assisted living to bridge the time until the end came. In these groups the barely animate were coddled and the pharmaceutical industry celebrated rich prophets.

There must have been plenty of patients in these groups who had purchased a new pair of athletic shoes for the sports classes here so they wouldn't make too much noise while working out. That turned out to be a waste of good money. For all the movement the corpulent, decrepit codgers could manage, they might as well have been wearing wooden boots with little bells attached to them.

Despite this, Angela came away from the experience with the opinion that it would have been better to consider the whole person when dividing the patients into groups, instead of simply rating them according to watts, even if this meant taking more time to consider the patients' needs. A smidgen more individuality would have been a welcome bonus, and it might even have helped to develop a better feeling of togetherness in the teams.

Because of their poor condition and the advice and encouragement the sports therapists gave them, many of the patients from the various exercise groups were probably thinking, Hey, where did all of these pounds come from all of a sudden? I don't get it. But heck, with lots of regular exercise, I'm sure I can get back down to a good weight in no more than, say, fifteen years. That would be quite an accomplishment.

Angela chose a group that concentrated on abs, legs, and buns, and allowed her to work with dumbbells sometimes, though the heaviest dumbbells they had were unfortunately only five pounds.

When she joined the group, she was more than a little surprised at the exorbitantly high proportion of men in it. In the world outside the House of Loose Screw Heads or Lunatic Castle with a Lakeside View, men largely avoided this particular kind of exercise class, but here in the Castle it was all the rage among the beta and gamma males.

Here men "in their best years" tried to work off their "Budweiser muscle." Men with slightly addled brains worked out here. The specialty of the house was men who looked like they were nine months pregnant. And let's not forget the men straining for a better figure who claimed to be hung like bulls, but probably only imagined that, having not been able to see around their guts to examine the facts for a very long time. Angela sometimes felt like playing the game "*I see something you don't see*".

She had seen the all brawn and no brains type in the abs, legs, and buns class, too. This category of man is easily identified by the lack of a neck, the lack of hair, and the lack of identifiable thought, though not always, and not necessarily all three together.

"Jeepers," said Angela to Molly, "have you looked over at the wall?"

There were nine men of widely diverse ages lined up at the wall performing stretching exercises, or at least trying to.

"Oh, yeah," replied Molly, and both began laughing out loud.

During many of the exercises these very same men invoked an image of a swarm of overweight ladybugs stuck to the wall and attempting ballet. What a thing to look at! What a vision of majesty!

Many of the men, but some of the women, also, only had their winter fat reserves from the years 1980 through 2012 to work off, which was frequently cause for great amusement for Angela and Molly.

The men in the class naturally hadn't noticed anything yet, hadn't registered that they themselves were the reason for Molly's and Angela's twittering, and probably couldn't imagine it anyway, so they threw themselves into trying to impress the ladies present. It was quite something to watch.

Molly, Angela, and the rest of the women naturally didn't let on to their true feelings, but rather let these overripe couch potatoes believe what they wanted, and even went so far as to lead them on with condescending smiles – the men, of course, didn't catch on to the condescension. It was cruel, but it was worth it to be a witness to this ongoing circus routine.

The twenty-five watt groups harbored the Neanderthal men. These hominids hadn't received the memo that excess body fat and a hanging gut were no longer considered the height of masculine allure in the twenty-first century.

The hair falling off of their heads landed on their shoulders and back, took root, and continued growing there.

My dear men, if you want to know how women want their men to look in this day and age, flip through the magazine *Men's Health*.

There are many businesses, for instance drug stores, perfumeries, department stores, and electronics stores that sell the equipment necessary for proper personal hygiene. This includes razors (electric or otherwise), epilators, wax, deodorant, cologne, etc.

Think of this as a well-meant tip from a friend, dear Neanderthal men! Modern women prefer well-groomed men, and are on the lookout for this masculine ideal. Well, at least they are out there in the real world. These were Angela's thoughts while observing the men in her class.

The addle-minded and the Neanderthals remained immune to the repulsed looks they were getting from those around them and stayed true to themselves.

Men in the beginning or sometimes advanced stages of

balding, who had bound their remaining, thinning hair in a ponytail, Michelin women and men, and tree hugging latter day hippies were at peace with their overly casual, jarring appearance that bordered on effrontery and could discern no compelling reason to change.

Some of the inadequately intellectually gifted were, as a consolation prize of sorts, blessed with a fleece that would have made Jason envious. Angela was just dying to suggest the solution to two of their problems at once: "Comb your chest and back hair and put it on your head."

Alas, all of these people wished to remain as they were. No wonder they couldn't get along with their neighbors back at home.

There was another group of interest that Angela happened to belong to: the cardio cyclists. This group exercised in a special purpose cardio room. Some of the patients in this group had known heart problems. They were strapped to an EKG for their own safety as well as the security of Castle management. These begrudgingly bound patients were monitored the whole time they were pedaling.

On the stationary bicycle "tours", the men liked to show off what they had. Some of the men in the group mercilessly rolled up their T-shirts to show the women their own version of the ideal masculine body. Good God, groaned Angela inwardly when confronted with this picture. Today really is a good day to die. Does this species have no sense of shame? Has it lost all decency? She had a different view of what it meant to be attractive. Angela and the other women stood facing eight bulging, wooly bellies.

Regardless of any feelings the women might have about it, these kings among men graphically displayed what they thought they possessed: sex appeal.

Unfortunately, these men had yet to comprehend that they had arrived in the twenty-first century and their bloated, fleshy, rotund bodies were now a hindrance in the selection of a mate.

Here one could see far too much of what one normally only wanted to see in an auto repair parts store: spare tires, spare tires, spare tires.

Angela noticed that her shoes had become untied during the exercise hour. She sat down on a bench while tying her shoes and thought: the Michelin man is really only funny in the advertisements, just like a jellyfish is really only mobile in the water.

In the twenty-first century, too much fat is no longer a signal of a good provider. Quite the opposite, in fact. Sorry, boys.

Fat is not beautiful, fat doesn't equate with success, fat does not make for a good choice. Too bad you arrived on the scene a few thousand years too late, my dear men, because nowadays women in the forty plus demographic still have the right to expect a certain minimum standard from their prospective partners.

Besides ideal women, field hand women, laundry women, cleaning women, and plain old housewives, there also happen to be emancipated, educated, unyielding, independent, demanding women.

Regretably, it seemed up for debate whether this latter type of woman wished to employ those attributes here in the Castle for which she had been fighting for the last few centuries, no, millennia.

Angela got up off the bench, bemused, and left the exercise room to look for Molly.

All Princes and Princesses

Dear princes, dear princesses,

Greasy hair, a large gut, leg hair, armpit hair, and hair on other visible and invisible body parts are a turn off in real life.

Angela and Molly got the undeniable impression that some of their fellow "inmates" were secretly blow-up fetish dolls with a 65 gallon capacity, hiding their air valve in the middle of their backs. They had repeatedly observed that even the fattest candle had a wick, and that wick was calling out to be lit. You've got to hand it to those irrepressible animal instincts.

There were also those men here at Lunatic Castle with a Lakeside View who had drawn the short straw in life, the poor things. It wasn't just their physical size that was less than imposing; the manner in which they conducted themselves was mousy and unsure, completely devoid of a sense of presence. These fellows had to grab what little hair was left on their scalps before their receding hairline receded into nothingness. They had obviously noticed the first stages of hair loss. They had not only lost an important head covering, but the poor guys also possessed only two brain cells, and each of these two brain cells remained uninformed of the other's existence, as was clear to the casual observer.

Looking upon these men, Angela couldn't help but think, Germany doesn't just have a problem with a declining birth rate; those few being born are also the wrong ones. These few new humans, lacking the cognitive ability to anything higher, immediately begin pursuing the opposite sex. Hope springs eternal in the human breast.

Those here were simultaneously disjunct from the rest of humanity and convinced of their own infallibility. They say everything has a name, but these people were indescribable.

"I wish I had whatever mirror they use," she commented to Molly. They were both standing in the entrance to the exercise room, casually looking around at the Castle, trying to avoid looking directly at the piteous sight of the underendowed men.

"Gosh," Angela sighed to Molly, "I would dearly love to feast my eyes, but naturally only my eyes, on a nice, normal man. I'm dreaming of the tall, dark, and handsome type: broad shoulders, muscular, fit, good smelling, intelligent, attentive, empathic, humorous, and charming."

This kind of man was exactly Angela's style. On a scale of one to ten, this was her idea of a ten.

"I may be older and married, but I'm not blind," Angela frankly reflected one day to Molly.

"I'm still allowed to dream. It doesn't matter where you get your appetite, as long as you eat at home. I may be married, but I'm not dead."

Molly began to laugh and they both walked into the exercise room together.

Pity and self-pity

or …
Everyone makes his own happiness

Molly and Angela were enjoying the first rays of sunlight together on a bench in front of the Castle, and were once again simultaneously observing their surroundings and the people in them with acumen.

"If the individuals here wish someday to experience happiness again in life, they will have to undergo serious changes in their behavior, their lives, and their physical appearance," commented Molly.

"Perhaps then they won't have need of all of the different medications and the perpetual stays in psychosomatic clinics. They could even rediscover joy in life out there in the real world!"

Molly turned her face to the early rays of the springtime sun.

The patients under discussion made certain that everyone, really everyone, knew all there was to know about their suffering. It was irrelevant whether the recipient of this free service wanted to hear about their tribulations or not; they griped for all they were worth. They were vexed when anyone patronized their lifelong trail of tears, or tried vainly to put it in perspective. What aggravated these energy vampires to no end, though, was when someone openly questioned their agony or their claims.

Here in Lunatic Castle there were men and women who simply couldn't cope with real life anymore, and preferred to hole themselves up in institutions like Lunatic Castle with a Lakeside View.

How "sick", how resigned did one have to be to reach that point!

"I wish they would stop trying to involve everyone, and I mean everyone, in their problems, if they're really doing that poorly. They're like sick octopi," fumed Angela.

She stood up from the bench they both had been sitting on with a "see you later."

She walked toward the entrance to her hotel so she could relax in her room some, clear her mind, feel her synapses slow down. Her goal was to flush her working memory.

Come on in, the water's fine!

or …
Splish splash …

Angela l knew that beauty is in the eye of the beholder, so she had trouble understanding the attitudes and reactions of her dear fellow female patients on their joint visits to water aerobics. Was she to understand that the other participants weren't quite as happy with themselves as they made themselves out to be at every opportunity that presented itself and some that didn't?

During their water aerobics classes these women couldn't refrain from dropping brilliant one-liners in Angela's direction such as "Did you just arrive from famine-stricken Somalia?" Or: "Real women have curves."

Or: "Men aren't dogs; they like meat on bones."

Only these – let's be gracious and call them modern day models for Ruben – were truly sensual women and not just fat.

This hospitable welcome from the harpies provoked her to leave water aerobics after a few short minutes. She wanted to beat a hasty retreat and not suffer the slings and arrows, the incisive looks, the caustic jibes from these "full-blooded women."

Where is your much-touted tolerance? You want to be accepted for what you are, too. Who appointed you judge and jury over me or any other woman who fails to meet the ideal weight or even an average weight for women? thought Angela, as she hurriedly dressed after her aborted attempt at water aerobics.

It seemed everything was a bit different here at Lunatic Castle with a Lakeside View. She felt like Alice in Wonderland. Everything here was offbeat, odd, a distorted version of the real world.

Angela was forced to admit that her own opinion of her body before the incident in water aerobics was up for reevaluation. She had considered her body entirely normal up until that point.

After taking a shower, she took a long, hard look at herself from all sides in the full-length mirror in the bathroom. No, everything was fine. Everything was right where it was supposed to be.

"That's good, old girl," she breathed in relief at her mirror image.

On a bad day, however, the mirror told her a very different story, and none too quietly. On those days the catty remarks about being too skinny from the other women in water aerobics seemed far from the truth.

She was the victim of an exercise deficit after three weeks here. At home in her customary fitness club she worked out at least three times a week for two hours. In the Castle her workout was lukewarm at best: only one hour at half-power. Because of this, her bad days in front of the mirror reflected a plausible image of her body, to her way of seeing things. She thought she perceived a lengthening of the skin under her triceps … wobble, wobble. This was her deeply held opinion on bad mirror days.

Besides the pool for water aerobics, there was also a very nice indoor swimming pool. It had Venetian paintings on the walls and ceiling and panorama windows that gave the patients a breathtaking view of the forest. There was absolutely nothing to complain about here.

In order to use the swimming pool and the sauna, you needed permission from the doctor and the sports therapist. If you were given permission, you received an X in your purple folded card that indicated such, and away you went. The road to the curiosity cabinet was open.

Almost every patient of Lunatic Castle yearned for the X that would allow them to use the swimming pool and the sauna.

What easier way to accommodate the meat market, the unending human bazaar? You could be scanned virtually free of textiles. What joy! What pleasure!

Despite having the doctor's and sports therapist's permission to visit the sauna, Angela never did. She had heard unpleasant rumors.

Why should she partake in the meat market of estrogen pumps with cup sizes ranging from double A to double D and testosterone bombs with a phallus length between three and eleven inches when she had a very satisfying number of inches sitting at home waiting for her?

Her husband Tyler was very well endowed. She really couldn't complain on that score. What reason could she possibly have to subject herself to the misery of the meat market? Why slurp out of a sink when she could drink champagne out of a crystal goblet?

In the swimming pool, just as in the exercise room, the swimming groups were divided by wattage, and the resulting jumbles of people made the consequences of this policy quite visible.

The sixty plus generation and the couch potatoes were in the twenty-five watt group, the fifty watt group was populated with a mixture of different midrange fitness levels, and the seventy-five watt group was the most delicious, its constituents having relatively well-trained bodies and the desire and will to really work out.

As soon as Angela walked into the indoor swimming pool, she felt the gazes of the other participants boring into her skin.

The stares of the other women, of whom eighty percent were full-bodied and wore clothing with cup sizes up to double D, made her uncomfortable, even if gravity had obviously taken its toll on the double D's.

Some of the females here must certainly have wished they could be models for swimwear, if it weren't for that little problem of losing weight.

Yes, feeling the other patients, male and female, gawk at her, and having to present herself before them wearing a bikini, sent a shiver down Angela's spine.

She felt as though she were on a presentation platter. It's your own fault, she chastised herself. You wouldn't have it any other way. You simply had to have an X to visit the swimming pool and the sauna … and now you're getting your just desserts.

The male swimmers present carried about "baby bumps" that gave them the appearance of being somewhere between the third and eighth month in a chimerical pregnancy. This was the best these muscle men could offer on the meat market.

Any pot-bellied pig would have been seized by jealousy upon descrying the corpulence on display here.

These Body Mass Index disadvantaged men shamelessly displayed their incomprehensibly repellant profiles to any females who made the mistake of glancing in their direction, and played up their counterfeit of attractiveness. These were precisely the masculine figures who were now analyzing Angela, just as some of the women were. They asked her how it was that she only weighed one hundred twenty pounds. "Jeez, girl, you need to eat more," remarked many of the men.

As everywhere in the Castle, the only goal for the men and women here was to scan for available objects of passion. As soon as a good one, or at least a passable one, was found, swimming ground to a dead halt. The swimming pool summarily became superfluous.

For example, water gymnastics might as well have been over as soon as a potential mate was sighted. The pre-adolescent giggling had already begun. Instead, foam swim noodles, floating balls, or other implements of underwater exercise found their way into the pool, for these were suitable toys for flirting.

Splish, splash.

Obviously some of the male patients no longer fit for work regressed to their time swimming in the uterus, to their prenatal development.

Women and men swam around the pool like flotsam and jetsam and looked like a swarm of drugged gnats. Angela saw men wearing veritable friendship bracelets as swimsuits.

Was Borat the fashion consultant here?

Many of the other patients had demonstrated their extraordinary taste in form and color in the selection of their swimsuits.

Angela couldn't have imagined that something so aberrant lay in wait for her here in the indoor swimming pool when she applied for permission to use it. Such a shame, really. She felt displaced and unsettled here, and was violently averse to appearing on the radars of any of the splashing, randy turkeys lurking in the pool. She wished she could remain in stealth mode and go undetected.

Because of the impressions she took with her from her first visit to the indoor swimming pool, she never returned there in her following weeks at the Castle. It was too bad, because the swimming pool was otherwise lovely.

She seldom saw happier faces in Lunatic Castle with a Lakeside View than the ones she saw in the swimming pool.

The old saying was true: there are two sides to every coin.

It's all a matter of perspective

or …
Self-perception and social perception

Molly and Angela wonderingly accepted that many of the men and women were obviously happy with their … uncommon figures. Molly and Angela, on the other hand, weren't always at peace with their figures.

Some days, for example, Angela thought, My body is a constant plague; I might as well be Sisyphus rolling a boulder up a hill. Once, her mental self-flagellation took this turn: There was a government initiative not long ago to get old cars off the streets and make way for newer ones. They obviously failed when it comes to me. Why am I still allowed out in traffic?

She even found her own image in the mirror alien on some days.

Some mornings upon getting up she would ask her reflection: What are you doing here? Shouldn't we know each other better if you're sleeping in my hotel room?

It was also entirely possible that she would look in her mirror and think: Two children. It's obvious. That's self-perception for you.

The two of them increasingly noticed that for many of the washed-up male patients and some of the female patients here, there was often a large gap between self-perception and social perception.

Angela and Molly could tell that many of the men in Lunatic Castle with a Lakeside View constantly had to re-estimate their market value. They obviously approached their reflections distinctly differently than the women in residence at the Castle.

These men hadn't noticed that they weren't Ferraris, but rather Yugos. They hadn't comprehended that they were not Godiva chocolates from a fine chocolatier, but rather jujubes from the corner grocer.

"I wouldn't think of trying to park a double-decker bus in a garage built for a VW Bug," Angela commented to Molly as they were once again blessed with the sight of male patients strutting about with swollen chests like wild turkeys in the forest during mating time.

It was noticeable that their chests swelled as soon as a forest fairy who sparked their imagination crossed their paths.

"Repeatedly having to hold their breath and pull in their stomachs to expand their chests … how tiring. We must pity the poor things." Molly laughed to Angela.

Since smoking was strictly prohibited in all of the buildings and living areas in Lunatic Castle with a Lakeside View, the entrance to, or the exit from, the Castle unceasingly looked like the misty entrance, or exit, of a haunted house.

You had to be able to put up with a lot, because the smokers gathered here to slake their addiction, or, if you asked them, to socialize with comrades, and the niveau of the mental flatulence they released on those surrounding them directly matched their ocular magnetism.

The genera represented here were wearers of gold chains, devoted Mallorca tourists (discernable by their loud mouths, small gold chains, and Buddha bellies), Ruben's models, Michelin men and pill-shaped women, and hairy male and female werewolves.

It must be said of the Castle, that one could live out every fetish, every eccentricity here. Yes, there was something for everyone here, if one wanted to find it.

It was an "audience" that was otherwise only assembled during the peak time slots of proletarian television.

Last but not least, there was the "normal" smoker. Depending on which of the four smoker's enclaves was currently being frequented the most, entering or exiting the host building could be either tolerable or downright unpleasant.

What made the whole thing worse was that the smokers only assembled in front of the buildings like this during wet weather. Should it precipitate, you could be sure that entering and exiting buildings would be like running a gauntlet; the assembled smokers were obviously afraid of water. Angela addressed one of the smokers while waiting for Molly right outside of one of the buildings:

"Hey, your smoke is bothering me. You're holding your cigarette so that the smoke always blows into my face."

This brilliant northern star actually had the gall to answer: "So it bothers you. Someday it will kill me, but you don't see me going on about it."

"What should I make of an answer like that," Angela had to ask. Molly, who had appeared in the meantime, was shocked by this intellectual phlegm. If it wasn't raining, the smokers liked to cluster together on the benches in front of Lunatic Castle.

They collected in great numbers on the benches, sometimes even sitting on top of each other, and pretended they were the jury at a fashion show or beauty contest, so that every time you had to go to the therapy rooms in the main building you felt like you were walking down a catwalk instead of across a yard.

Not one of the patients was spared this humiliating gaping and rating. After passing by this self-appointed jury for involuntary appraisal, you got to hear the flattering comments of the constituent men and some of the women as well. "Not bad." "Don't walk so fast, or we can't get a good look at you!"

"Did you see the one with the big tits? I'll bet she's wild on the dance floor … or in bed!"

"The tanks are rolling again."

And on and on in the same demeaning manner.

"Since you have the crappy karma of ending up as walking assholes, someday, somewhere you can expect to be covered with shit." Angela shot back one time when she was the addressee of one of these comments.

Dear lobotomized men, dear emotionally under-ripe women, dear sufferers of an allergic response to intelligence, these comments strengthen the self-assurance and self-esteem of the other patients like nothing else! You are true heroes! Our country needs more people just like you – NOT!

"Women already lacking in self-consciousness will doubtless lose the last remnants of self-consciousness they had after rehabilitation here," fumed Angela and considered Molly thoughtfully.

Molly and Angela were just leaving the main building after lunch when the makeshift jury once again dropped its snarky analysis like bombs on a war zone. I never forget a face, thought Angela, but in your case I will be delighted to make an exception.

Angela and Molly became enraged when they spoke together of the fresh antics of the gamma men and Michelin women. "They've undoubtedly all been watching too much television – most probably one of the currently popular reality television shows featuring rising models. They think they've learned that unkind, biting commentary is a boon to society. Don't these simple-minded fools realize what effect their rude comments have? Don't they understand that they are being destructive and leaving a big mess behind them? 'Big mess' is too mild. Ruins or landscapes pockmarked with craters is more like it." Molly vented to Angela while enjoying a cigarette. There was no escaping the assessment, critique, and judgment here in the Castle.

It was too bad that the mirrors in the rooms of the self-appointed jury members must have been permanently broken, or perhaps they were magic fairy tale mirrors, or maybe they had been brought in from the fun-house at the last carnival and they bent the image of every slob such that he looked like the pick of the litter.

Oh, well. Not every woman can be a princess, thought Angela as she stepped into her room. She had been forced to this conclusion even though she used to believe just the opposite, namely, that every woman really is a princess, but some haven't yet found their princes.

Angela was still sunk in thought as she laid out her clothes for dinner with some pride. Jealousy is given freely, but pity must be earned, she thought, as she changed for the evening meal.

The earth-dwellers who arrived a few days after Angela, the so-called newcomers, were interesting as well. Among the new admissions there were also some self-styled "understanders of women", and they had their own methods for coming into contact with the women of their choosing.

The espied, the chosen, the favored were either sized up the whole time they were taking a meal in the cafeteria, or one of God's gifts to women approached the object of his interest after one of the group sessions. Molly and Angela had been subjected to this a few times, themselves.

One tried the following opening on Molly:

"How much longer will you be here?"

To which he received the reply:

"I don't know what business of yours that is." Angela was handed.

"Have you made any friends yet?", to which she riposted …

"I didn't know I was looking for any."

On another occasion when she was leaving the therapy room with Molly and a man from her therapy group named Thomas, the latter addressed her with this question: "So, have you gotten settled into Lunatic Castle?"

"What do you mean," Angela wanted to know. "In what way, exactly, am I supposed to settle in? My time as a guest here wasn't entirely voluntary. My health insurer sent me a letter politely but firmly requesting me to check in to this clinic." "Sure," said the bird of paradise, "and perhaps I should have worded the question differently. Have you mentally arrived? I'm dying to know whether you feel at home here, whether you can identify with the therapy sessions offered here in the Castle, and what you think of the other patients, what your estimation of them is."

Angela gave her fellow group member a questioning look. "Concerning your first question: Are you really interested? Besides that, where am I supposed to have arrived?

In myself?

In the Castle?

In this quaint little town?

In my room?

In the hotel?

As to your second question, I think you've presumed far too much in asking. What makes you think I want to talk to you about the other patients?"

"You don't believe that I'm interested in your thoughts?" Asked Thomas.

"Believing something requires a minimum of interest in the question at hand," Angela answered, annoyed.

How pathetic, she thought, and wished only to board the waiting elevator as quickly as possible. For once, she didn't have to wait on the blasted thing like every other time. It was waiting on her for a change. She got in hastily to avoid having to answer any further questions.

The next subculture in the Castle was the men who were forever young. In real life they were upwards of fifty and hadn't achieved much of anything during that time in the outside world. Now they had reclaimed their teenage years. Alternately, there were a scant few men checked in here who really had done something with their lives to date in the real world, but behind the portcullis they wanted to test the waters again. Perhaps they wanted to prove that they weren't fossils yet, took the saying "you're only as old as you feel" to heart, and felt themselves back to twenty or slightly older. Being that young again allowed them to search out and acquire living, breathing Barbie dolls here on the grounds: great figure, pretty face, small brain. They were the best things that could happen to these men. The aforementioned women were easy prey for men such as these who aim no higher than age twenty-one, give or take a year.

The women, girls really, who were approached by the suddenly youthful men (at least they imagined they had just stepped out of the fountain of youth through their association with the young women) giggled and gesticulated like there was no tomorrow. One was only left to hope that the obviously pea-sized brains of all involved would grow someday.

Angela had the feeling that intelligence was doggedly pursuing many of these needy groups of Castle inmates. The men, woman, and girls were always faster, though, and so intelligence never had a chance to catch up with them.

While observing this group of people, Angela had a sudden vision of a note that read:

"A day without you is like a month of vacation.

I know you need me, but I'm sorry; I had to leave. I was ripe for a vacation. – Your brain."

Although the brain is not a muscle, the patients at the Castle and their sports therapists were at such pains to heighten physical fitness, it seems a shame that they would neglect mental fitness and let the brain atrophy. Much like muscles, the brain should be trained daily to keep it in good working shape.

If one were to allow oneself an evil thought, one might wonder what had been accomplished by the overdose of Viagra presumably necessary for these mismatched couples to function in bed. And if, perchance, one allowed oneself to continue down the path embarked upon by this first evil thought that led behind the bedroom door of these lovebirds, one might wonder what happened when they then played doctor together. The mutual surprise might have been quite something at a crucial point during foreplay when form enhancing, form reducing, or infirmity concealing clothing was removed. Something like finding the prize in a Crackerjack box, but perhaps not as pleasing.

Yes, these ruminations would only be possible for a dark, wicked mind. Too late.

Then there were the ceaselessly parched patients – let's call them the sex-deprived patients. They would choose a woman to approach and ask her out to the movies, for example. If she refused, this kind of man would move on to the next woman. According to Angela's observations from afar and personal experience, the next woman was always the same type of woman as the last one. Thus, this kind of man turned right around and asked the next woman of the same genus he saw once he had been brushed off by his previous choice.

Should the next woman be equally uninterested in a date with him, that was no problem. Fresh blood arrived three days a week. Tuesday through Thursday new arrivals poured in, and they could continue to strive for their lofty goal until on one of these days they were finally able to snag a fresh hunk of meat.

Their principal of operation was that sooner or later this method had to be successful, had to net them what they wanted.

This was confirmation enough that women always looked for the right man, but men could experience pleasure with any woman, even the wrong one.

Incomprehensible, but the continued success of these men justified their belief and thus their method. Dearly beloved men, such conduct is definitely not nice! And women: not every man is a prince who wishes to sweep you up onto his steed and carry you, his comely maid, to his castle to rule with him. These were Angela's thoughts as once again she watched one of these men put his moves on a woman.

Dear men, each woman is unique and should be treated that way. Every woman is a princess and cannot be returned to the service counter in a department store for a replacement after she has been used once. Dear men, please remember that on your next hunting trips. In many cultures, myths, and religions our world is called "Mother Earth," because this is a powerful and appropriate image of fertility and life as the omphalos of the human experience, opined Angela as she brooded over the recent events she had witnessed.

It almost made Angela sick to her stomach to think about how every even marginally attractive woman here constantly had to fend off the advances of various of these, let's not kid ourselves, sex-hungry men. The image of the fat little ladybugs on the wall sprang up once again in her conscious mind.

If a woman had received and rejected an offer from one of these men, or even gone so far as to let it be known that she was not on the market and not interested in such propositions, she was thenceforth branded as arrogant, bitchy, and stuck up.

These were clear cases of self-centeredness built on a foundation of narcissism.

Dear men, life is not a long string of missions of reconnaissance and conquest into the realm of women. You don't get everything you want in life.

"You have to have a woman. All that counts is that she's alive," Angela overheard on one occasion. "Put a bag over her head, if you have to."

"Women are nothing more than half-dead objects."

"You know, some women think 'breast cancer' is one of the signs of the zodiac."

These were other such winning statements made by real, live men in the Castle, as overheard by Angela and Molly on their exploratory walks through Lunatic Castle with a Lakeside View. "Pea-brained idiots," Angela complained to Molly.

"That's just the way of things." Angela lamented to Molly.

"No one acquires reason automatically. Those who deny her cannot be conquered by her."

Angela and Molly were conversing on one of their tours of Lunatic Castle when Angela said, "Oh, dear male patients, you beautify every room you pass through by leaving it. What kind of complex must you Hercules wannabes feel compelled to compensate for that would make you resort to such base machinations and verbal warfare? I can't imagine all of the things that must have gone wrong in your lives.

Thank heaven you're now in the House of Loose Screw Heads in Bad Kleeblatt, where you can discuss all of your deficits, your fears, your concerns, and your needs, in short, your entire emotional condition, in group and individual therapy sessions." Molly looked askance at Angela and said to her: "You think about a lot of queer things."

The patients who were so bored, they didn't know what to do

with themselves were another special treat. This group managed to avoid the therapy sessions offered by the Castle. They spent their time sitting in the three available waiting and reading rooms in Lunatic Castle with a Lakeside View.

This "team" was in agreement that they only travelled as a pack.

They observed the world and the people around them, evaluated it all, then doused those passing by, or, more accurately, those hurrying by, with their demeaning comments. Better still, this tribe tried to convince those hastening by their territory to take part in their speculations and senseless conversation, to partake of their sophomoric drivel. If the passerby didn't wish to participate, they were treated to a free sample of said drivel.

Admittedly, this was a way to deviate from generally accepted conventions for establishing contact between humans. Yes, it was far from the norm, grating really, but why not? This was one way of putting the desired and widely touted tolerance toward differences supposedly present in the general populace to the test. After all, these attempts by the pack to make contact with those trying to avoid them required nerves of steel.

Whenever possible, people tried to avoid these rooms. Unfortunately, this wasn't always possible, but anyone who still possessed a modicum of consciousness, who was still playing with a full deck, who didn't have any screws loose, tried anyway.

The differences couldn't have been bigger

or …
Variety is the spice of life

Angela was shocked, or frightened, or, on closer inspection maybe simply irritated by the mixture of humans who were allowed to stay here together for four, six, or eight weeks. There were groups for all of the various ailments the patients suffered from, and she was no exception with her condition. The possibilities included roleplaying, self-help groups, and so on. Angela loved calling it gruesome grouping. These choices were offered on top of the sundry forms of occupational therapy everyone participated in.

A substantial percentage of the jewels of creation, otherwise known as the female patients, were spiritual beings. More than a few of them believed they were angels, or if not angels themselves, then at least ambassadors of the angels, transporting the words of the angels directly from their mouths to the unwashed masses.

How sad.

Angela could hardly keep a straight face while conversing with these women. What could possibly have happened to them in life that this phenomenon of near self-deification was so pronounced among the women in attendance?

All sarcasm aside, she heard some truly appalling personal histories that nudged her toward the beginning of a long overdue reevaluation of her own life, past and present. They caused her to see her life in a new light, and be thankful for it, despite all of the travails she had had to face.

The vicarious experiences she endured through the other patients' tales of sorrow in self-help groups and group therapy, as well as her own relived experiences, and the resulting insights gained from individual therapy were easily one of the best things she could take with her from her stay in rehab back to her everyday life.

The mixture of patients included transsexuals, who wanted to, ought to, and needed to redefine their calling and their place in life. They were just as well represented as the hard-core lesbians, the sadomasochistic gays, and the sex addicts.

As soon as the diagnosis "sex addiction" had been heard, people began to smirk behind their hands, but what these sick people, who were no longer able to control their sexual desires, had suffered … friendships fell apart, contact with co-workers, neighbors, and other people of significance was strained and unnatural.

These humans fell into a black hole, caught in limbo, and became depressive on top of it all because of the misunderstandings and lack of tolerance, lack of acceptance, quite simply the lack of knowledge about this illness.

Angela hadn't known previous to her experience here that this addiction, this sickness was accompanied by such manifold consequences.

There were burn-out patients here, and cancer patients, too, who were here to drag themselves out of the abyss and back into a fulfilled life, who were here to learn about viewing their torments through a different lens, who were here to put things in a new perspective and learn how to adjust their lives to accommodate these debilitating illnesses. Besides these groups of people, common housewives and mothers who had been bled dry by the roles they played came to Lunatic Castle with a Lakeside View to fight their depression and start down a new path toward self-actualization.

Also among those reframing their past here at Lunatic Castle with a Lakeside View were former soldiers suffering from post-traumatic stress disorder. Hearing their stories and emotionally trying to put herself in their shoes was unbelievably horrific for Angela.

The explanations and explicit, visual descriptions achingly given by one of the former defenders of our nation overtaxed Angela's capacity for emotional stress more than once.

His tales of his tours of duty in Afghanistan, Congo, modern day Croatia, and off the coast of the Ivory Coast in an anti-pirating division were thankfully beyond the powers of her imagination.

The ordeals he lived through on these tours of duty shocked Angela and doubtless many of the other group members. This one man had lived through more than anyone should be forced to endure!

Another group of people Angela met during her stay here for the first time were androgynous life forms. These gender-neutral residents had the problem that their very lack of gender caused them to interact differently with other people, and this was met by limited acceptance and tolerance by those closest to them. That led to the onset of ennui. They were visiting the therapy sessions and other forms of assistance in the Castle to regain the will to live and learn to deal with the lack of acceptance from their fellow human beings, while learning to accept themselves for what they were.

Besides all these groups of people, there were also the victims of rape. The perpetrators did not distinguish between genders. Angela was horrified to discover that the abuser was often a family member of the victim. The former victims, who had grown up in the meantime, were trying to understand their past and, as much as possible, put it behind them.

Angela was very interested in a very different, special group of patients: the ones who had come with their imaginary friends. There were a few of these in the Castle. They were charming people, and very, very entertaining. It was nice to have them as a contrast to the previously detailed fates.

The last group of patients was those in mourning. Into these groups gathered the pained souls who couldn't carry on with life after the death of a loved one, who simply couldn't cope with the loss. They had lost a part of themselves in the process. They were here to learn to accept what had happened, to understand it, and to come to terms with it.

Then there was the exceptional case of one member of the stronger sex and his summons to the Castle. This patient had been caught behind the wheel on a traffic camera after indulging in a visit to an establishment with free refills on beer. After the storm of flashes from the traffic cameras and the resulting photographs he had clearly been discredited. He had received so many demerit points on his traffic record that he had not simply had to take a psychological examination, as is mandated by German law after a certain number of demerit points, but had supposedly been required to move into Lunatic Castle for a trial period.

That incorrigible man.

He said he was here for a Functional Ability Evaluation. Was that his true reason for being there? Well, everyone has to learn his or her limits when it comes to alcohol. Still, Angela doubted his story, for she had never heard of a stay in a psychosomatic rehabilitation clinic being required after drunk driving. But if this hombre thought it was the truth, so what? It was no skin off of anybody's nose if it wasn't true.

And once again she heard that incredulous voice in her head asking: "What did I get myself into?"

The day before, she had spoken to another woman here who was actually convinced that ghosts resided in her house.

She could converse with the ghosts living in her house. Yes, this head-turningly attractive woman had explained, very convincingly, by the way, that she had made contact with the ghosts living in her house, and asked them for advice on problems in her life.

"Angela," said the Eve of the Castle, "whether you believe it or not, I live in a one family house. The house is very old, and when my second husband was on business trips there was always creaking and clattering and other strange noises. When I went to find out what was making the noises, I never saw anything for a long time.

One evening when it was already very late I was sitting in my living room feeling miserable.

I felt alone, and I was despairing. I should tell you that I've been suffering from depression for years – ever since the death of my first husband. Suddenly I felt like someone was standing behind me.

I felt a light breeze and something like a soft touch on my

right shoulder. Later, I left the living room for just a moment to get something to drink, and when I returned, a photo album that had been lying on the coffee table was open to a page with family pictures from happier times when my first husband was still alive.

I remembered those times, that warm feeling, the wonderful hours together during which the pictures were taken, and I immediately felt much better. In the time since that first encounter I've grown accustomed to asking my ghost, or maybe ghosts, for advice when I feel bad, when I don't know what to do, but I don't want to talk to my second husband about my problems or my worries and needs. They have, or perhaps he has, thus far always given me an answer to my question."

How exactly a meeting looked between the ghost or ghosts and Lilly, for that was the name of this Eve of the Castle, was more than Angela could bring herself to inquire. The whole thing was too intricate for her.

It was really time for Angela to go home. The first thing that occurred to her on hearing Lilly's story was that she had seen a movie in the theater once about paranormal phenomena that reminded her of this. Associating the story Lilly had related to her with a movie was indication enough for her that she had been here too long.

Introduction to the many forms of therapy

or …
What some people can, want to, should do to keep busy

More than a few of the other patients were thrilled with dance therapy. Those participating gushed about the success they had had with this form of therapy. On such high recommendation, Angela decided she would try it out, too.

The first time she appeared in the group, she instantly recognized that she didn't belong here.

Many of the people here were surely graduates of a Waldorf education.

These now-grown children probably got sick of their environmentally conscious parents' narrow-mindedness, and they went out in search of new ways of making a name for themselves. The dance therapist looked to Angela to be in the same category, and her teaching methods reflected that. That's not to say that that kind of teaching is inferior – not at all. Angela, however, could not identify with the style of communication or the teaching techniques employed. She was obviously too much a part of the here and now to open herself up to this style of learning.

The "dance lesson" had hardly started when the dance therapist excitedly, almost euphorically ejaculated: "Dance your anger, your fury, your fear, and all of the other feelings you're contending with out of your body! Get grounded, feel yourself, your ego, your body, your spirit, your soul! Hug a tree! Lie down in a field of flowers!"

Help! Help! thought Angela.

Her tolerance was being tested at maximum thrust.

This was definitely not her group. Twelve men and women danced back and forth all across the room. Every one of them danced in their own way, many of them wept, shivered, collapsed, whimpered, or screamed. Whether this happened before, during, or after hugging the imaginary tree, or before, during, or after lying down in the imaginary field of flowers remained a mystery to Angela.

She stood somewhat off to the side and longed for the end of the dance hour. She had never seen anything more bizarre.

She felt like she had landed in the middle of the movie "One Flew Over the Cuckoo's Nest".

When was the movie's main character set to arrive? Was he already here, hiding among the dancers, or perhaps skulking in a dark corner of the room?

The topical groups – we'll call them that for lack of a better name – were also worthy of note. In these groups, clinical pictures based on the current conditions of the participants were analyzed.

For instance, the patients living with depression heard about the different classifications and forms of depression. Appropriate medications with their active ingredients and their effects were explained. The diverse forms of therapy available during the progression of various illnesses were outlined, then presented in detail. Topical flip charts were created and presented by the patients themselves. Participation on the part of those unfit for work, which was everyone, was actively encouraged.

The topical group sessions took place weekly.

Fortunately for Angela and Molly, they were assigned to the same topical group by their respective therapists. They were taken aback upon discovering that they were the only two patients present who were not strengthening their currently weakened personalities or changing their personalities altogether through the application of medication.

Both therapist and pill-popping patients bandied about their knowledge of antidepressants, as they're known in the medical community, which only served to alienate Angela and Molly further.

Details about effects and dosage were exchanged much as wine connoisseurs discuss vineyards, vintages, aftertaste, clarity, storage, and bouquet. The resulting scene was absurd!

For fear they would be the victims of a verbal siege by the rest of the group, Angela and Molly concealed their refusal, their absentation from ingesting any antipsychotics, any colorful happy-makers, anything to get them to drop all of their inhibitions.

Right now, they didn't want to confess their unwillingness. You can never be too careful.

Besides with Molly, Angela only spoke with the therapists in individual therapy and with her doctor about her refusal to take antipsychotics.

During her entire time in Lunatic Castle she had gotten the impression that this would be interpreted as a judgment of the other patients, and she didn't feel that was fair to them as human beings.

But wait: there were more forms of therapy available, such as ergotherapy. Ergotherapy came from the catalog of tools borne of occupational therapy, and was just as interesting as the other therapy options at Lunatic Castle with a Lakeside View.

The things you could undertake to do in this course were widely varied!

A list of the activities from which to choose was placed where all could see it. The possibilities were: jewelry making, basket weaving, sewing clothing for dolls, painting, pottery, carving soapstone, and making a teddy bear.

For those who had not yet come into contact with that most outlandish new contraption, the computer, the opportunity was now available. This clutch of patients could, sometimes had to, often wanted to use this chance to make first contact. These candidates could now establish an intimate relationship with this novel technology.

Angela couldn't help but think: We're in the twenty-first century. There can't be more than a handful of people who don't know how to use a computer. Is it even worth offering this class?

But she was sadly mistaken in her assumption. The class could accommodate ten to twelve people, and it was always booked solid.

Well, well. Even here one could draw one's own conclusions based on the massive influx of intellectuals.

By the way, the chances of evading the incredible, phenomenal course offerings that were part of ergotherapy were zilch! Every inhabitant of Lunatic Castle with a Lakeside View was lovingly assigned to one of the ergotherapy groups. There was only one option left up to the patients: pick your poison.

Besides the computer course, all of the courses could accommodate up to seven participants.

One had to give the therapists credit: they were all very motivated.

Yes, they were all so terribly nice and attentive. They gave great effort to making the patients' time in therapy as pleasant as possible, for the sessions often ran over the strict thirty minutes allotted. The groups were so lovely, the therapists were quickly willing to give of themselves and extend the session to forty-five minutes for the sake of the patients in attendance.

Angela had thought thus far that this kind of therapy was only offered in the workshops for the handicapped, but during her time in Lunatic Castle, she was taught a thing or two.

Individual therapy was also offered in this group, but Angela didn't even want to know what that looked like.

To round out the "shopping cart," there were autogenous group exercises. The group members could learn how to let themselves fall into a form of trance, meditation, or relaxation when they encountered stressful situations in their every day lives. Those with temporarily attenuated faculties were to take wing and escape from the grind of their everyday lives for a few minutes. They learned breathing and relaxation exercises that would carry them to the land of their dreams. One could, or should, imagine an island, a sky full of stars, or something similar, and use that as a portal through which to begin one's journey to one's inner self.

But what a disgrace! How many times had some of the gamma males and full-blooded females fallen asleep in autogenous therapy?

Only after the loud snoring on the part of the indisposed participants became too much for the otherwise motivated therapist did she directly address those responsible, and demand more active, honest engagement! What a show!

The therapist's demand went something like this:

"Harvey, I hate to interrupt your sleep, but it would be a real shame to miss out on the experience you can gain in my course, to get nothing out of it for your personal development, just because you fell asleep. Please concentrate and take an active roll in the course starting immediately. We'll all thank you for it."

Now, wait a minute, thought Angela after this slap on the wrist. Who told you that I would thank him for his active participation? Maybe I would sooner thank him for the sporadic interruptions to your arid course.

To imagine that this reprimand would be embarrassing to those caught dozing would be a mistake. Decency and morality were barred at the portcullis to Lunatic Castle with a Lakeside View, or rather, most of the ailing newcomers gladly shed this heavy burden at the gate.

There were precious few exceptions to the rule that the inhabitants here were not integral, not good examples, not proper, faulty, without a conscience, and shameless. Whoever had not recognized or chose not to recognize this, whoever still put their faith in or hoped for virtuousness, decorum, character, and consideration from their fellow human beings, whoever believed that a community or connectedness existed here at the Castle, was either a fool or a dreamer, as far as Angela could discern.

It would be a grave omission and fail to do justice to the entire range of therapy offered if breathing exercises, spinal exercises, art therapy, Qigong, progressive muscle relaxation, and body memories were not mentioned.

And let's not forget topical group therapy, individual therapy, the different possibilities in the various sports therapies, and discussion groups in the wide repertoire available.

Topical groups

or …
Group terrorization in the panic room

In spite of all of the foregoing, Angela had heard a number of very, very serious life stories that wouldn't give her any peace.

For example, the stories of political refugees – people made sick by their dreadful experiences in their home countries outside of the European Union. Men and women alike were condemned to such fates. She had met utterly traumatized men and women here at Lunatic Castle who were trying to work through their experiences.

Secretly, she hoped that they could do that; that those suffering from trauma would receive the help they needed here to leave their pain in the past.

Confronted with these fates, she realized for the first time how trifling her problems truly were in comparison.

Maybe you can imagine the mixture of patients and what group therapy in the topical groups looked like.

The therapy sessions, incidentally, encompassed at least ninety minutes each. A few times Angela and the rest of the group members stayed a good two hours. It was a well-mixed group of adults, and she had the privilege of enjoying the group feeling that had developed three or four times a week.

Men and women in this group began to cry out of the blue. A box of tissues stood always at the ready for these crybabies, in case they should need it. Angela was not exempt from these weeping episodes. The mood in the group was so depressed on some days, that Angela thought, If someone doesn't provide us with a breath of fresh air, I don't want to know what could happen …

On other days, some of the comrades rushed out of the room as if they had ants in their pants, a few were silent and withdrawn, some smiled ceaselessly, and still others simply started to laugh out loud for no observable reason.

One of the other female patients in Angela's topical group said one day, "I have constant problems with the world around me. I think the people in my social vicinity don't see me for who I really am."

"What do you mean by that, Nicole," asked the therapist.

"Please tell us exactly where you see the problem and what you mean by your statement."

"Well, I rub everyone the wrong way," elaborated Nicole, "all of my acquaintances quickly fall apart, and it's all because I tell people the truth. I tell them what I observe, I tell them the things I notice about them and their behavior, and I tell them what I don't like about them."

"What are you trying to tell us right now?", asked Henning.

"Do you mean that you overdo it?", inquired Ina.

"No, no, not at all. I just think it's awfully strenuous that those around me don't understand that I'm always right and they're not. That what I say is always exactly what is. That my comments are always correct."

"Are you trying to say that everyone else is wrong and only you are always right? That you always see things from the correct perspective?"

Angela could hardly hide the irritation in her voice.

"Yes, that's exactly what I mean. I'm the only truly complete and perfect woman in the world," retorted Nicole, and she challenged the whole group with her glare. She honestly meant the trash, the baloney she was spewing.

Everyone in the group therapy room had to let this verbal assault on reason and compassion settle for a few minutes, but after a while the therapist broke the silence. "What a stressful thing to imagine that all other humans are incomplete, and you yourself are the one perfect being on the whole planet. Never questioning yourself, and going through life with the notion that you have always done everything right, and will continue indefinitely to do so. Always looking for fault in everyone else, never believing yourself to be capable of making mistakes, and so never looking inside yourself or at yourself in the social mirror. Never viewing yourself critically saves you from facing the things you shouldn't have done, but also bars you from seeking forgiveness and healing for them."

Believe it or not, when the therapist was done calmly and respectfully presenting these thoughts, Nicole stood up without a further word, without even deigning to glace at the group, shot out of the room, and for the rest of Angela's stay was not seen in the topical group again.

Angela discovered later that Nicole had gone to her individual therapist after this incident and complained bitterly about the impudence of the group therapist. How dare he hold up a mirror to her like that in front of the group!

Nicole subsequently joined another group, then another, and another, and so on. She changed groups another four times during her stay at Lunatic Castle, since she could never seem to find acceptance for her off-the-wall views in any of the other groups.

On top of that, the grapevine, which worked exceptionally well at the Castle, informed Angela that Nicole was a hard-core lesbian. She hated every last man on Earth, sight unseen. Angela figured that the key to Nicole's difficulties likely was intertwined with some experience with men out of her past.

A was confused when one day the therapist of her topical group therapy declared he could not bring himself to participate in the group interactions on that day. He didn't feel himself to be capable of it at the moment.

The topical therapy session that day took place in a room that was fairly new and unaccustomed for the therapist.

He explained to the group that he couldn't actively participate for the following reason: the carpeting, which Angela considered nothing more than a typical throw rug, made him arrecho.

A-ha. The carpet, or throw rug, had made him arrecho.

Angela's curiosity was aroused, so she googled "arrecho," just to improve her vocabulary, of course, and came up with the following synonyms, among others: horny, randy, sexually aroused, sex-obsessed, willing, erect, hot.

Amazing. Based on one statement on the part of the therapist, it became clear what the kind of throw rug one might find in Wal-Mart, the kind of throw rug that had no adverse effects on Angela, could awaken in a person.

The changes in social behavior, or any other behavior, on the part of the poor therapists resulting from working in a psychosomatic clinic for decades were laid out in the open for all to see. This particular topical group therapist was one of the psychologists who had been working in Lunatic Castle the longest. Could this be interpreted as confirmation of one of the prejudices coursing through the general public against the psychologists working in psychosomatic clinics?

During another topical group therapy session Angela witnessed another confession worthy of note. One of the men in the group whined that he didn't feel confident enough to give the irritating man in the room next to his a piece of his mind. The poor thing.

This group member was according to his own testimony a former policeman and a former soldier, and was now a government employee with a severely dysfunctional relationship to his superior.

He didn't believe that women belonged in positions of leadership. His boss was new and female, and that contributed to the tremendous psychological pressure he was under, and was indeed one of the primary reasons that this man had felt it necessary to check in to the Castle. Angela's theory was that this member of their clan had been raised on a strict diet of yoghurt and right-wing politics.

This Bubba was six feet one inch tall, weighed an estimated 330 pounds, had arrived in his midlife years, said he was only forty-two years old, had shaved his head bald, and had an unusual, puffy face. Perhaps alcohol was part of the puzzle. Angela didn't know, and it was none of her business. This was definitely not her problem to solve.

At least this guy had no bad hair days.

His dress was out of the ordinary: black jogging pants; flip-flops; short, tight, black T-shirts; and to complete the cliché, a black windbreaker. He wore this stylish ensemble and followed his own terribly attractive dress code for the entire time Angela lingered in the Castle.

Angela had the feeling that he might fly off the handle at the slightest provocation.

This man wasn't exactly the poster boy for Aryan supremacy.

It was, however, precisely this man who claimed to need harmony and sought good advice from the group. Well, well.

The group spent almost ninety minutes giving him advice.

If this is the worst of the problems this crew has …, thought Angela after the session was finally over.

During another session on a different topical group therapy terror day, another man from the group related to the others present that he and his relatives had reportedly had an inherited debt of seven hundred thousand euros dumped on them. It would be next to impossible to pay off this debt in their lifetimes. How in God's name could one dig oneself out of the pit of a seven hundred thousand euro debt? Could his story even be believed? Why wouldn't one simply turn down an inherited debt in that order of magnitude? Angela sat on her seat contemplating the situation and looking questioningly at the man.

Oh, well. Life is full of consequences, and that which is cannot be argued into nonexistence, thought Angela. If the claims forwarded by this man were true, a proposition that tested Angela's capacity for trust, then this man had a knack for landing up shit creek without a paddle.

The man who had entrusted his tale of misfortune to the group looked down-and-out for sure, and lacked basic social graces. He was generous with his cussing, tirades, and worse.

He had a degree in business administration.

A-ha. So he was a failed business administrator. He certainly should have been able to do figures … He had worked for a temp agency as a helping hand in a warehouse for years purportedly because he couldn't find work in his field. Could it be that this man had read too many fairy tales? Or mayhap sniffed too much glue?

Or had he simply not taken his uppers yet today? Hadn't had any "vitamins" that make the world so much more colorful, no antidepressants, and so he was left relating this steaming heap of contradictions to the motley crew assembled.

Besides the therapist, a doctor in his induction year attended the group therapy sessions in Angela's topical group. He took his turn on one day bemoaning the miserable working conditions for doctors and therapists. It was just a crying shame that Angela had almost lost her life to a planned operation and the incompetence of the person operating on her.

Angela had to endure quite a few further operations to save life and limb (literally) as a consequence of the doctor's malpractice during the planned operation. She had been confined to a bed for weeks in a hospital in the capital of Schleswig-Holstein (a little state in the north of Germany). It was only thanks to her new doctor after the operation, who reacted to her situation quickly and transferred her to the hospital in Kiel and into the care of a team of doctors headed by an excellent professor, that she was still present and accounted for.

But she was still condemned to live out the rest of her life with permanent handicaps to life as she had known it. She had to learn to rearrange her life around the new and decidedly different lifestyle mandated by the situation thrust upon her.

Since the series of operations, she hadn't slept through a single night. She was trapped in her own movie, which bore the title "You Only Live Twice". Every night at two in the morning, give or take a few minutes, she woke up for the first time. It didn't matter when she went to bed: midnight, earlier, whatever. She always woke up for the first time at the same time. Every hour after that, she woke up again. Her nights were short.

She was shaken by nightmares every single night in which she experienced her own death, over and over again, in the most gruesome ways imaginable. The doctors and therapists had diagnosed her with trauma. And now this superficial crybaby actually expected sympathy from her for the conditions in his working day?

Besides her sleep disorder and trauma, she also sustained lasting damage to her leg due to the series of events surrounding her failed operation. Her leg was marred for the rest of her life, and her foot not fully functional. She couldn't just wear a skirt any time she wanted, or she would be constantly aware of the curious looks of passersby.

Angela was furious after the group horror was over, and fled the torture chamber as quickly as she could to avoid saying something she would regret.

She met Molly in one of the Castle's hallways and had to let off steam.

"He really should have done his homework. He should have reviewed the group members' files first. One would think it would even have been enough simply to pay attention to what I had said in the discussion previous to his diatribe. What an exemplary doctor! His depth of empathy has surely never been equaled. His career as a healer of body and soul is assured," Angela quietly seethed at Molly, nearly frothing at the mouth.

"Calm down. Let's go have a cup of coffee together. After that, the world will look very different.

You'll see," Molly pacified Angela.

"Yeah, okay, if you think it's a good idea," Angela grumbled.

They went toward the café next to Lunatic Castle with a Lakeside View. The café was famous not so much for the coffee and cake they served as for the immoderate prices for which they served them. Thus far both of the women had always detoured around the café, but today was a good day to help prop up the recessive economy.

Angela had experienced something today in the core therapy group that she would just as soon not have experienced, and that she called:

Group terrorization in the panic room!

On this day she had learned that very important people will never be an endangered species on this planet.

The therapist who guided her group did not agree with the old saying "think before you speak," no, no. He was of the opinion that one should speak first, then think. What a brilliant philosophy.

As far as Angela was concerned, this led to nothing but chaotic discussions in the topical group therapy sessions.
Some of the group members had immediately taken this well-meant advice from the therapist, his brilliant new philosophy, and put it into practice by insulting and hectoring the other group members to no end.

To Angela's astonishment, the therapist had sat by and done nothing. Quite the opposite, in fact: when one group member got up in a huff to leave the room, the therapist creaked into action and finally convinced the person to stay.

Angela's stay in Lunatic Castle with a Lakeside View had once again irreversibly altered her view of the world.

This very same therapist had repeated confidential information in front of the whole group that one of the group members had related to him tête-à-tête in an individual therapy session.

Angela couldn't imagine how this could be reconciled with doctor-patient confidentiality. It certainly took getting used to on her part, to say the least. It felt unnatural. It was sad testimony that one stopped caring as much as this man had obviously stopped caring after over twenty-five years of service in a psychosomatic clinic, she thought as she looked out the window, lost in thought.

It was really too bad that new problems were created this way instead of helping to solve old problems. Angela seriously doubted that this was productive or even constructive.

She had been with her husband Tyler since 1976 without a pause. Just like everyone else, they had had their fair share of highs and lows in that time, but she could truly claim to be happy with her husband. They had been leading life together as a married couple since 1980.

He was her friend, the father of their two fantastic sons, her lover, and yes, her life partner.

After all those years, Angela still liked being with him. She discussed all of her problems with him (when she had any), was proud of him, and even got jealous of his behavior around other women. She stayed with him because she wanted to stay with him, and couldn't imagine life without him.

Consequently, she held the audacious opinion that she was really, truly, and with all of her heart happy in her relationship.

It was customary for everyone to introduce themselves the first time a topical group met. A few weeks previous, during this introductory round through the group, Angela had introduced herself and had had the chutzpa to mention her familial standing and the so-called happiness she associated with it. Her words were, verbatim:

"I'm happily married and have two healthy children."

Another group member, Frank, immediately jumped all over her for this statement.

"Sure," said Frank, "but I just have to wonder if you're really happy. I think we should hear what the rest of the group has to say about that. What do all of you think? Now that Angela has introduced herself and officially let us partake of her happiness, can you imagine her as being happy? After all, she felt compelled to make certain we knew this."

"You've got to be kidding me. How screwed up do you have to be ..." She started to ask her opponent. She couldn't bring herself to complete the sentence, but did manage to project a calm and collected image to the outside world. She was fuming inside, though, and was speechless at his impudence.

Please note, dear reader, that she had never met this man, Frank, before her introduction to the group. Angela had never had the privilege of exchanging pleasantries with him before this moment.

Where is the therapist to rein this man in? she asked herself. He was sitting placidly and without comment in his chair, possessing the temperament of a frozen reptile, and displaying obvious amusement at the scene playing out before his eyes.

He didn't twitch, didn't make the slightest movement to shoo Frank back into the hole he had crawled out of. He simply let Frank try to tear apart her credibility in front of the group.

Frank then had the brazenness to detain her after the group session so he could talk over everything with her, get to know her better, and finally to apologize for his behavior during the gruesome grouping. He admitted he had overdone it.

What a self-righteous bastard! Was all Angela could think during this encounter.

This ultra-important man arrogantly informed her while looking at her down the full length of his nose that he was trying to gather impressions of all of the group members, including her, so he could figure them out.

How important can one imagine oneself to be? She didn't want another patient trying to figure her out. What on Earth is this man thinking? Angela asked herself more than once. This poor sap had to compensate for his inferiority complex with arrogance and the way he treated other people. He fed his inferiority complex by exposing, discrediting, making fun of, and deriding other people.

There were many more disagreeable clashes to come between Frank the self-righteous bastard and other group members.

When Angela pressured him later in one of the group sessions, he haltingly and grudgingly admitted that he had landed in social services after going through retraining and completing a second education.

Now he was charged with the care of difficult teenagers.

What are social services doing to our children? Angela wondered as she looked at this man.

Comment: This very same self-important idiot appeared to have well-developed muscles on one hand – his right hand – from the forward and backward motions of his hand gymnastics. He must be right-handed, thought Angela as she noticed the very visibly over-developed muscles of his right hand.

He didn't seem to be happily married. The poor thing.

She understood from later discussions that her deduction about Frank being in an unhappy marriage was dead on.

I hope to God you're one of a kind! she thought as she looked at Frank, and put in an additional prayer that the rest of humanity was hoping the same thing.

Old age can be so nice

or …
When life's second springtime calls

Another day, another horror.

Angela had hardly arrived for her cardiovascular workout in the stationary bike group when her comrades in arms from the group trotted in.

Among others, there was a Krusty the Clown lookalike, complete with cigarette; half of a retirement community; and old super machos who still couldn't come to terms with their real ages, and loved to knock ten or fifteen years off for their reported ages when they were required to introduce themselves.

This last group, the gang that hung out with Krusty, felt that here in the rehab clinic they were being given their very last chance to find a partner, and they were intent on not wasting that chance! The feeling that every time might well be the last time gave this species a strong sense of urgency and led them to show off whenever and wherever they could.

This caravan of old men wanted to show the world what they had one last time. They had set the goal for themselves of proving their mettle to everyone, or, more correctly, to all of the "attractive" women. They, the antediluvian men, were not really old. And they most decidedly had not lost their relevance in this world. They were here to convert the entire female population in the Castle to this conception of them! Many of them meant the word "conception" in a very literal sense!

The old women being courted, for they were at least fifteen to twenty years older than Angela herself, built a towering wall of dignity around themselves just to see how high the old suitors could jump.

Not a bad tactic.

Collected impressions

or …
Oh, and by the way …

Angela had already been on the stationary bicycle for half an hour.

On this particular workout day an old macho hombre sidled up to her from the right and brayed in her ear: "What are you trying to do? Ride all the way home? At that speed, you should be there soon!"

Angela had always believed that everyone enjoyed participating in sports. She was now in the midst of a crisis of belief that had its origin in her experiences here at the Castle.

What is your problem, she thought, but she simply answered, "I'm not sure what exactly you're trying to tell me."

This Free Willy was obviously in heat.

He was sniffing the water for mating scents coming from the females in his vicinity. This beached whale actually tried to continue the conversation after Angela's clear brush off.

"Well, it's not every day that I see someone like you here in Lunatic Castle."

This was probably intended as a compliment.

If this hadn't left her speechless, she wouldn't have known what to say. After a few seconds of being dumbstruck, Angela replied, "I choose to construe the statement you just made as a compliment. I hope it was intended that way." What she was really thinking was, what a mind-numbingly below average come-on.

She hoped that he had understood her rejection, underscored by her fitting body language in his direction, and that she would be left alone by this septuagenarian at least for a few days, and preferably for the remaining weeks of her stay.

It was a nice dream, but this particular dream didn't come true. This man, who to judge by his mummy-like appearance had certainly painted the town red with the Pharaoh, showed no mercy. He had tasted blood. The universe was visibly breathing new vigor into the husk of a body he had remaining.

The very next day this same wild turkey tried to strike up a conversation with her, and abused her with his lascivious stares.

Don't you see that I'm not interested? she thought.
She continued to concentrate on her peddling speed while listening to one of the original German comedians on her iPod – a great and famous comedian of the first order who never wearied of amusing her.

This amusement allowed her to tune out her surroundings and escape the visual holocaust confronting her every moment she spent in the workout room. She probably laughed out loud more often than people were used to from her. She chuckled out of pure enjoyment, which aroused the sports therapist's attention.

Yes, Angela had unintentionally diverted the therapist's focus to her personage. It wasn't long in coming that the therapist addressed her concerning her vocalizations of pleasure. "Well, Angela? Having fun today?"

Yes, yes, one was never left unobserved in Lunatic Castle with a Lakeside View.

Big Brother is watching you.

The scene is now a different day in the bicycle sports group.

Angela was sitting on her cardio bike when the head of the sports therapy division entered the room. She had reportedly had great success in a national sports team of some sort in her best years. The way she behaved, the way she bore herself left the distinct impression that despite her seemingly advanced age of approximately somewhere in her mid sixties, although Angela had heard tell that she was really only at the end of her fifties, she still clung to the golden days, still mourned the lost fame and glamor she had basked in during better times.

Said head of the sports therapy division ran through the workout room like Speedy Gonzalez, made a beeline for the windows without any prior announcement or inquiry, and tore them open. Then she hastened back out of the room as quickly as she had come without a single syllable of explanation, salutation, or interrogation in the direction of the patients present, who had now had a new climatic condition forced upon them. Indeed, she did not even deign return their inquisitive looks.

It surely goes without mention that she did not consider it worthy of her effort or attention to close the door to the workout room behind her as she left.

The result was, of course, that all of the lightly clad, sweaty cyclists were left in the middle of a powerful draft.

It would have been polite to ask the high performance athletes if she should provide for some fresh air upon entering the room and deciding that the oxygen content in the air was no longer sufficient for those present, and the smell wasn't precisely springtime fresh, either. After receiving an affirmative response, she would have been welcome to crack a window or two. What a great diplomat she was! What a priceless treasure!

Many of the course participants could have quickly caught a cold after her attack if the therapist on duty hadn't had the presence of mind to jump up and close all five of the windows that had been left fully open as well as the door.

Yes, aging gracefully is tricky, Angela thought, upon reflecting on the head of sports therapy's performance. The good woman surely wouldn't have tarnished her crown if she had treated the patients present with the respect they deserved.

What bug had gotten up that dear woman's ass on the day recounted? Who had died and made her God?

The head of the sports therapy division was obviously just as well loved among her colleagues as among the patients.

The other therapists cringed and quaked when they encountered her, and any conversation that was taking place when she entered the room promptly came to a halt.

This came as no surprise to Angela, for the head therapist had built a formidable wall of arrogance and aloofness around herself.

The battle of the buffet

or …
Angela I's daily fight for survival

No less impressive than the rest of the visible establishment were the hallways to the cafeterias, created in style with marble and decorated in taste with demure paintings. And no less disappointing than in every other physical space of these stately surroundings was the conduct of its inhabitants. It was too much to expect comportment from the mentally ill more amenable to general society than the abysmal and downright rude manners that passed for etiquette here.

Once one had arrived in the cafeteria, one had a good half an hour to shovel food down one's gullet. Imagine some one hundred seventy people, all of whom were convinced that this would be the last meal they would ever eat, and you have a good idea of what you would see in both cafeterias in Lunatic Castle with a Lakeside View in Bad Kleeblatt.

Angela and the other patients were greeted every morning and every evening of their stay in Lunatic Castle with the sight of a buffet.

The prospect of grazing on a buffet for two of three meals every day sounded heavenly upon checking in on the first day, but it turned out to be a challenge twice every day during her rehabilitation.

One morning she was standing in line to get a breakfast roll when quick as lightening another patient's arm squeezed through the line, snaked past her from behind her on the right, and landed on the buffet in front of her. The hand attached to this arm snatched the last two breakfast rolls left in the basket right in front of Angela.

The miscreant clearly considered the tongs in the basket to be nothing more than decoration. To be fair, it should be mentioned that in order to use the tongs properly, in order to operate them as designed, the pushy glutton would have had to get in the back of the line, just like Angela and the rest of the convoy of the starving had done.

Angela loved to have a salad from the salad bar with her dinner.

Angela was standing in line with all of the other hungry souls when she experienced déjà vu. Once again, a phantom hand shot past her from behind and through the rest of the line and grabbed a ladle that was in a large container of salad dressing at the buffet. Owing to the blatant misuse of the ladle, its contents did not land on the desired object, presumably salad, but instead unfortunately slopped all over Angela's sleeve.

If you imagine that the person responsible excused himself, you would be wrong. There was no apology for not being able to wait, no apology for not getting in line and waiting his turn like everyone else, and no apology for drenching another patient's sleeve in dressing.

He showed no trace of remorse. After all, Angela had been in his way, and thus had no one to blame for the incident, for her misery, but herself. All she had to do was step aside for this nice young man so he could get everything he needed to stuff his face. His action clearly demanded retaliation from Angela. She just didn't know how and where yet. But they would assuredly meet again while at Lunatic Castle with a Lakeside View.

There were days when her stomach remained so empty, she could have wolfed down an entire cow, because if you didn't arrive on time for a meal, mere minutes late made all the difference, you could be out of luck – the buffet may already have been picked clean.

How she missed home at moments like these!

Were she at home, she would have only to go to the refrigerator any time she wanted, she could eat whatever she felt like tasting, and, best of all, she wouldn't have to fear having her food swiped out from in front of her and devoured before her eyes.

No one would spill food or condiments that she didn't want all over her.

No vultures would hover over her meat, and no hyenas would be waiting to see what she brought back from the hunt.

Good table manners must be learned

or …
Could you use a cheat sheet of etiquette?

People dressed up for dinner, but the same fallacy was applied for dinner dress as at any other time: less is more.

Fifty to sixty year old seductresses wore clothing they had obviously borrowed from their eighteen to twenty-five-year-old daughters.

Men wore their pants somewhat lower than their hips, and often wore tight sweaters or T-shirts. All in all, the clothing they wore was very … form fitting.

Many of the patients proved that good taste was truly in the eye of the beholder.

Good taste is the ability to persistently oppose excesses. Praise be to those who tried …

The visual accompaniment did nothing for Angela's appetite. Enjoy your meal!

One evening Angela sat at the table and carried on a conversation with the person sitting across from her.

She was quite sure that this man could understand, yes, even absorb what she was saying. She got the impression that he also kept himself free of happy pills, that he didn't take any reality-enhancing psychotropic substances. He was just as clean and Renate and herself, at least as far as she knew.

The man sitting across from her was an older gentleman with the pleasant-sounding name Thomas. He was almost old enough to retire. He was only here because he had reached an agreement with his employer: Thomas wanted to retire early, but needed some time off before that, and his employer had accommodated these two needs.

He had helped care for his own mother many years, and immediately following that he had done the same for his mother-in-law. His internal batteries were so drained that he needed a much longer time to recharge and return his former capacity for the usual level of performance.

Besides Angela and Thomas, Elisa, Sofia, Matthew, Adam, and Mary all sat at the same table together. This bunch of people always took meals together.

Mary, who sat diagonally across from Angela, sprang out of her seat one day completely without warning, and stormed out of the cafeteria, only to return some time later with something in her hand.

She raced around the table toward Angela to show her a teddy bear about two feet in height. Angela was confused but she politely admired the bear.

But seriously, how grotesque a scene when a woman in her mid-fifties jumps out of her seat at the dinner table right in the middle of a discussion and without forewarning as if stung by a bee, hastens out of the cafeteria, returns to the communal table twenty minutes later with a teddy bear in her hand, and presents this worn out stuffed animal to another patient as her lifelong companion, beaming all the while!

Clever businessmen

or …
How stupid can you be …

The village of Bad Kleeblatt lies close by the lakeside Castle.

Around ten minutes of easy walking took one from the Castle to the village. It was no surprise that plenty of businessmen lacking in scruples attempted to serve the market created by the patients of the Castle.

Within a radius of about one mile around the castle, you could hardly spit without hitting a store purporting to be for all things spiritual in which you could buy angels, amulets, crosses, pendulums, singing bowls, essential oils, incense sticks, books about the rites and rituals of magic, and so on.

Courses were offered so the purchasers of the aforementioned wares could better orient themselves in the world of spirituality. Angela could no longer count how many such courses were available.

Beyond that, there were stores where you could have tarot cards read for you, or your future told.

There was a plethora of advisors for life's problems, water diviners, spiritual healers, séance mediums, feng shui consultants, esoteric career consultants, and other very successful merchants.

Those who were good at crafts were not deprived of the attention lavished on the residents of the Castle, either. There were multitudinous stores to cater to their interests as well.

Many shop owners sold wool, cloth, thread, etc., including, of course, the necessary implements to use them. Among other things, this included knitting needles, sewing needles, crochet hooks, and so on. These rounded out the wares for sale.

It goes without saying that these stores also offered courses fitting to their inventory, such as knitting, sewing and crochet. A different course was offered every week.

The street leading up to the Castle grounds reminded Angela of a Turkish bazaar. One year previous, she had been in Istanbul. The great bazaar there was comparable to the goods and services being hawked here.

Cheap products were sold at unconscionable prices. Here, in this market place in a free market economy, the law of the free market truly did govern. The Gross Metropolitan Product of Bad Kleeblatt was definitely bolstered by the patients of Lunatic Castle with a Lakeside View.

Collectively, there was a lot of divining by pendulum, knitting, sewing, crocheting, tarot card reading, and soothsaying in the Castle!

Some of the more intelligent patients struck upon the lovely idea of relaxing themselves in the evening with incense. After all, they had bought it, so they had to use it. Too bad all of the rooms were equipped with smoke alarms.

If one was not interested in submerging oneself in the world of New Age spirituality, that was no problem for the assiduous businessmen.

The enterprising shop owners had found a further, equally lucrative market: beauty and health. Hordes of cosmeticians, masseuses, and physiotherapists opened their doors wide to the waiting public! There must have been twenty to thirty of each. Admittedly, these salons and practices had spectacular offers.

A bit farther on, the pizzerias, wineshops, and pastry shops, as well as restaurants serving good old German, or Asian, or Italian, or Croatian, or Turkish cuisine were crowded together, having long since smelled good profits.

This throng of businesses competing for every euro and the people trying to squeeze by each other reminded Angela of Disney World during peak season.

The restaurant owners who had set up shop here had a great day every day due to the famine that prevailed at Lunatic Castle with a Lakeside View on an unbelievable number of days resulting from an unmitigated emptiness that predominated the buffets.

Business boomed for all of the restaurateurs, bartenders, pizza bakers, kebab joints, rotisseries, and so forth because of all of the starving clientele who only just managed to drag their grossly undernourished bodies from one meal at the Castle to a second round in the city and plunked down a pretty penny for these emergency rations.

The high density of patients compared to residents in the village (for every sixty residents there were doubtless three or four patients) kept this area of business in full bloom.

It was no surprise, then, that there were overweeningly flashy, pretentious luxury cars in front of more than a few of these establishments, presumably owned by the same people who owned the stores themselves.

The absolute dedication on the part of the shop owners to their own fiduciary well-being above all other principals infused Angela with a morbid respect for their single-minded pursuit of their own highest goal.

Angela simply found it appalling that a callous money machine had been set in motion to feed off of the sickness, the fears, the worries, and the needs of many patients.

When nature calls

or …
The call of the wild

The patients of this internment camp of the ill were permitted to make use of the lakeside area around the lake right next to the Castle. They could, for example, walk all the way around the lake, jog around it, swim in it, or just take a casual stroll on its shore, depending on their momentary personal disposition.

Even in this otherwise pastoral landscape, there were plenty of enterprising businesspeople. Paddleboats in every shape and color imaginable were available in large numbers to be rented. They had a paddleboat in the shape of a swan, a "regular" paddleboat, a duck-shaped paddleboat, one that looked like a car, and many more figures besides.

There were three inviting, comparatively large cafés along the shore that were good for a leisurely hour or two. On sunny days, these cafés were goldmines.

At one location along the edge of the lake there were even facilities set up for accommodating swimmers, and one could pay to use the lake as a pool, even though one could get to the lake from all sides, and there were plenty of places where sand had been dumped on the shore to create a beach. At these other locations, swimming in the lake was, of course, free … Yes, it's all a matter of turning a profit.

The lake was not big. One complete circuit around the lake took a good hour for someone in decent physical condition.

This round could easily be completed by a physically healthy middle-aged adult walking at an average pace in that time.

The most fascinating sight in these beautiful natural surroundings, though, were the many, let's call them "natural events".

The lake was right next to a small wooded area. Everything here in the House of Loose Screw Heads that had found companionship tested the lakeside woods as a place to become closer still, weather permitting. People were boffing each other left and right.

Long dormant floods of hormones were once again set in motion here. The old ball-and-chain at home was replaced with a newer model here.

There were so many people being nailed here, their hammers were in danger of falling apart.

No kidding: collective moans and cries of pleasure drifted up from the woods.

Since the lake and the entire piece of property surrounding it belonged to the county, there was nothing the rehabilitation clinic could do to prohibit this group coitus.

Since swimming in the lake was permitted, this offer was regretably often taken by patients one wouldn't want to espy in swimming suits, swimming trunks, or, worst of all, in bikinis. Those patients who would have filled the indoor pool all by themselves in Lunatic Castle were here using the lake.

Completely pain free, these XXL swimmers put the fullness of their bodies on display sporting swimwear that had been designed for XS figures.

You don't always get what you want in life, thought Angela as she witnessed the atrocities to good taste so often flaunted here. You never have, and you never will.

Other cultures, other customs

or …
Adventures in a new world

Then there was the medium large group of patients originating from the Near East close to North Africa.

The patients from this group couldn't have been more different from one another. Exquisitely attractive young women sans head scarf were just as well represented here as devout wearers of the head scarf both young and old, fat and thin. Pious and not so pious men of a wide range of ages rounded out this group.

It must be noted that Lunatic Castle with a Lakeside View was very accommodating of these men and women, since many of these suffering souls could speak little to no German. There were, however, also some who could speak German very well.

Extra therapists and translators who came from the region in the Near East near North Africa, or at least had been raised with the language of that region, though born in Germany, were employed by the lakeside Castle to assist precisely these patients. The translators employed here understood and spoke the native language of their parents or grandparents. In this way, those men and women who otherwise would have understood little to nothing were able to participate in the verbal communication around them.

For no obviously rational reason many of the husbands of the women checked into Lunatic Castle with a Lakeside View could be found with them lounging in one of the break rooms all day every day. These husbands must have rented a room in the area in order to be there to "entertain" their wives during the day. One could only encounter these women without their husbands late in the evening. The reason for this was quite likely that the clinic closed at eight o'clock and could only be entered or exited through the main entrance. Partners of the patients of the lakeside Castle could spend the night with their partners, but for the privilege they had to pay room charges that were high enough to give one pause. Clearly, it was less expensive to rent a room in a nearby boarding house.

The question Angela found herself pondering again and again was why droves of women and men from the Near East close to North Africa, but more the Near East part, or rather from the Anatolian Plate, which borders the Eurasian Plate to the north and east, the Arabian Plate to the south, and the African Plate to the south-west, had marched into Bad Kleeblatt.

Indeed, they even paid full cost for their guest quarters in Lunatic Castle with a Lakeside View.

She discovered the answer to this question later in her topical group.

Some of the patients from these earthly latitudes residing here were political refugees, and, with help from the Castle therapists, were trying to come to terms with what they had experienced in their native lands.

It was interesting to observe that when this pack sat down at their favorite place to sit – on the Castle walls – the men and women sat separately, they pursued their hobbies separately, and most of the women submitted to the men.

The "herd mentality" was also quite visible. This picture prompted Angela to think, completely free of prejudice, of course: "*Back to the roots*".

Some of the patients from this culture were open and formed relationships with other patients. Mostly, though, the people from this culture kept to themselves. So much for immigration and integration.

Emancipation, or equal rights for women, was another issue. The men from said latitudes made their view on the subject clear through their actions: if the emancipation of men had worked for the last five thousand years, that shouldn't and needn't change now.

Emancipation of women? No, thank you!

It was really too bad, since these men and women were all very nice, but when together they behaved in ways that took us Westerners some getting used to.

Angela could observe nothing but loyalty and courtesy for the other patients from this group out of the sunny region near Africa. Indeed, they were exceptionally helpful and friendly.

It goes without saying that the women from these latitudes could never be found in the sauna, and only a handful of them ventured into the indoor swimming pool.

Angela and Molly philosophized together about the worldviews of the Islamic countries that were so strange to Westerners, and about the decidedly different view of women among the Muslims.

They decided that if the two groups, Westerners and Muslims, were to get closer, they could surely learn much from each other. Their conclusion was that an acquaintance or even friendship with women or men from the Near East would be a fantastically wonderful experience.

Our country needs new children

or …
Watch out! Kids!

Angela and Molly were always interested in watching mothers arrive with their children. Our future retirees. Childcare was available for this group so the suffering dams could participate in the therapy sessions and others groups without the chattering and cries for attention and love from their children.

"Children are the most wonderful and the biggest challenge on the planet. Once you've had them, you would never want to live without them. Once they're there, you can never get rid of them. You can't say to them, '*Go back to where you came from.*' You get what you ordered, and there are no guaranties, no escape clauses, and no returns. On top of all of that, the little scions cost an exorbitant amount of money and take up a hefty portion of the time you have in this life."

"Whoever has the fortune of having children knows what the two of us are talking about." Angela opined to Molly as they watched a caravan of mommies sitting outside the admissions office waiting to be processed.

The way some of the mothers treated their bundles of joy made Angela think that they really hadn't known that before they had had children. Why hadn't anyone warned them?

To make matters worse, Angela and Molly could see that many of the women present felt incapable of meeting the demands placed on them by their roles as mothers. The two Graces were just leaving a therapy session when Molly whispered to Angela,

“I should put a stop to these mothers yelling at their offspring by delivering a speech to them. ‘Dear mommies, this is a lifelong pact that you knowingly entered into; it seems safe to assume that you were present during the conception of your children. Or were your tikes all immaculately conceived? Just because even you have now noticed that your little terrors demand all of your love and attention is no reason to transform into violent Taliban mothers.”

Just precisely this group of obviously square pegs was given the privilege of dining in a specially designated, cozy room.

Angela didn’t believe for a minute that the intention was to make the mothers’ lives easier. Instead, she was fairly certain that all of the other patients were being “protected” from the mass of bearers of the genetic inheritance between newborn and school age. The little dears were noisy. It dawned on her that this might have been a way to avoid confrontation. The little urchins were brutally honest, and often wore their hearts on their tongues…

She found it so queer that so many young women came to stay at Lunatic Castle with a Lakeside View with their own flesh and blood.

By the by, during her stay she had not once seen a male patient with his progeny in the Castle. Was there a deeper meaning to that?

Angela felt endlessly sorry for the women and their young ones, but mostly for the latter. Why, oh why, thought Angela, don’t these poor mothers, these sick souls, receive any support from their families? From their husbands? Their partners? Their boyfriends?

Why did these women have to check in for a stay at the lakeside Castle with their snuggle bunnies? Were some of them looking for escape, for relief?

More than a few mommies were put on medication during their stay at the Castle to help them conquer their daily lives when back outside the portcullis again. But what would happen if those who had brought life into this world were taken off of their prescription medications? What would happen with the dams' mood swings? On the other side of the coin, how would the little ones adapt to deal with their mothers? Sad, sad, sad.

Angela couldn't bring herself to consider it further.

The sensible prescription of medication

or …
Hooray! I'm high!

It gave Angela pause that the men and women on prescription medication shuffled through the halls like zombies. Under the influence of antidepressants, they acquired a flat affect, or, as was not uncommon, slept through one or two days.

As some of the therapists said in conversations or informational presentations on the subject, the body needed a few days to adjust to taking new antipsychotics or no longer taking previous ones, and the outward behavior Angela was witnessing were "merely" side effects. These side effects were not pretty, but they could also not be avoided. The choice to be made was between sickness and health.

Well, if those weren't just marvelous choices. How lovely. How comforting.

Were these patients really on the path to healing through their use of anti-grouchiness pills or whatever it was they took, or had they simply been pacified, silenced, and placed in a hermetically sealed plastic bag for categorization and filing?

Angela wondered whether it was worth pawning the future and abandoning the present to obtain a chimerical and fleeting victory through oblivion. Every human can, of course, only answer this question for him or herself.

She was and remains positively certain that she would never be ready to be transformed into a "zombie" against her will and conviction. She would have to be diagnosed with something extreme, such as manic depression, before she would ever reach for pills of any kind. She had noticed that friend makers, antidepressants, were far too hastily prescribed for her taste.

She was horrified at the changes brought about by the happy makers to other patients in her topical therapy groups.

Angela considered this form of therapy more than questionable.

The therapists said that medication of this sort was only to be taken on a short-term basis, yes, but then why had so many of the other Castle inmates been on their drugs for years, or even decades in some cases?

When Angela asked one of the other female patients about her perpetual use of antipsychotics, she dissolved into tears and said, "I'm afraid of what I'll become if I stop taking the pills. My husband asked me not to stop taking them, because when I do, and I've tried it many times, I become quite different, become someone else entirely. He can only tolerate me when I'm on the pills. At least that's what he told me. Because I'm afraid of losing him, I keep taking the pills."

Angela was shocked to her core at what this relapsing patient had just spoken to her in confidence.

What an understanding gentleman the husband of this sick woman was!

Had it ever crossed this sick woman's mind that her husband might be her real problem?

Quite obviously the continued use of the good mood pills was based on a purely psychological dependency, and was intertwined with the fear of not being able to cope with life without the pills, and with a phobia of facing one's own life and its attendant problems.

Taking these "party pills" was clearly related to taking any other mood-enhancing drug: once taken, one was always on the lookout for the next kick, for the next trip, for the next journey to the land of freedom from pressure, fear, reality. Even if it was as was claimed, and these drugs did not create a physical dependency, Angela noticed that the psychological dependency was every bit as real, every bit as problematic, and every bit as tragic.

Good therapy, alternative medicine, or homeopathy were certainly further respectable options for treating the symptoms many of the people who had checked into the lakeside Castle displayed. Beyond that, psychological care from depth psychologists or behavioral therapists as well as self-help groups could be very meaningful and effective, and ought to be applied first to the more uncomplicated clinical pictures. That was her firm belief, anyway.

Angela could only reiterate to any psychologically sick human she knew that her own experience showed that you have to climb out of your own valley of lamentations, dig out of the Egyptian tomb that had been sealed with the curse of the pharaohs and break the curse.

Breaking the self-imposed chains of steel and returning to real life was worth the effort. Life can be a beautiful thing. You simply have to reacquire a sense for the beauty!

Out of pure self-interest you ought to re-sensitize your sensory organs!

How beautiful is the sound of a child's laugh, how melodious a birdsong, how warm the touch of the sun on your skin. How elevating it was to watch a sunrise, and equally sublime to gaze at the setting sun. What enchantment to savor the taste and smell of a well-crafted meal. What a singular experience to pause in the middle of everything with your face turned to a flower, close your eyes, and let go of everything but its fragrance for just a moment.

She could only entreat all of the afflicted to enjoy every day, every moment, to feel every beat of the pulse of life in their here and now.

You should never deprive yourself of the gift of seeing the world with your own eyes!

Carpe diem!

Angela's current residence

or …
Her bohemian shed

Angela lodged in the hotel on the waterfront next to Lunatic Castle with a Lakeside View.

Her home away from home was a tastefully decorated hotel room about two hundred fifteen square feet in size.

The room even had a black marble bathroom with a generously proportioned shower stall.

The room was furnished with a single bed; an ottoman made of leather for reclining; a leather armchair; a small, round, glass table; a chair with leather upholstery; and, not to be forgotten, two art deco floor lamps.

The room was equipped with a television, of course, but there was a catch. It was fairly small, and was only operational after you purchased a remote control from the hotel reception, much as is often done in hospitals. Angela supposed that this television was left over from a time when televisions were still newfangled, perhaps somewhere around 1935. At least it looked that way. At the very least it was certainly an old CRT.

The most attractive aspect of "her" room, though, was without a doubt the wardrobe. It was an eleven and a half foot long sliding door wardrobe. This was nothing short of pure luxury for a hotel room.

A large picture window allowing the eye to soak in a view of the lake was also a big plus for the room. How often had she crawled out of bed in the morning only to open the curtains, crawl back into bed, and watch the sun rise over the lake … This room, this vista made so many other things tolerable.

Just so her room met with excellent cleaning service, she bribed the cleaning personnel with a few euros in the hopes of better results. Much to her delight, her strategy worked quite as well as hoped, and she continued receiving premium service after the first and each of the subsequent bits of financial support, also known as tips. Just try saying that money can't buy happiness.

To her mild dismay, she did have to change her own bed sheets. Fresh sheets were placed in her room every week.

Being included in the daily tasks of a hotel employee must have been considered to have a pedagogical value. The hotel guests who were also guests of the Castle were obviously not to lose all of their self-sufficiency.

Perhaps it was on account of the years of collected professional experience on the part of the employees of the lakeside Castle that it was assumed that otherwise more of the patients would never become reacclimated to "normal" life.

Giving up the luxury available at the Castle of leading a life of dependence, mindlessness, and absolute paternalism was obviously more than some of the more morbid patients could take. For that reason, there were some patients who never again wanted to be without the opulence of never having to think, never having to decide, never having to take responsibility, and attempted to check into the House of loose screw Heads View again and again.

A visit from the head physician

or …
Angela's day before the tribunal

Well, well. Today was the big day. The head physician was coming for a visit. Right here and right now a tribunal of three doctors she had never met, the head physician, and a therapist she had never met would pass judgment over her return to the work world.

How comforting. She was excited and tense at the same time.

This gathering always took place three weeks after arrival. At least that was what she had been told, or, rather, what had been insinuated to her with all the attendant rumors. Those would be that the tribunal could instantly tell the difference between the hypochondriacs and those who were truly suffering, that the tribunal employed questions below the belt, and so on.

It was all over; she had withstood the visit from the head physician. Contrary to her apprehensions and the lurking dread instilled in her by the whispered suppositions and shreds of conversation half overheard and half invented, the visit had been quite satisfactory.

The head physician, whose acquaintance she had previously made, as well as the other doctors present and the therapist were each and every one very nice, empathic, friendly, and polite.

These were not attributes she ascribed to every psychologist in Lunatic Castle with a Lakeside View.

Angela could go home soon. They spoke of one or two more weeks' stay, then au revoir, arrivederci, hasta la vista, sayonara, and good-bye!

That's what the head physician told her.

After the visit, she started daydreaming.

She jubilated over the news she had been waiting for since nearly the moment she had arrived, and returned to her hotel room with a spring in her step to find her mobile phone and call all of her loved ones so she could share this triumph with them.

A paucity of information

or …
It's good we talked about this

Now that Angela had tarried in the lakeside Castle for three weeks, she was informed by her sports therapist for the very first time that since she seemed to enjoy exercise so much she was free to use the stationary bicycle for a full hour.

It had never occurred to the therapist to mention this earlier? Wow!

It was a perfect demonstration of how humble one became behind the portcullis and its corollary, how thrilling tiny accessions were when one had been reduced to a minimum of autonomy.

Today was truly a good day.

Angela peddled happily on the bike.

For one whole hour.

That is, for fully sixty marvelous minutes.

Weighing in

or …
Minding your girth

This can't be. On this particular day, Angela had found a note in her room mandating an appointment to be weighed. She was to appear at the nurses' station before seven in the morning the next day to stand on the scales.

Angela hadn't the slightest intention of actually going.

She had been admitted as a guest at the Castle because she was the victim of medical malpractice, and she was now quartered here solely so her return to the work world could be decided upon. That was it. She had not been admitted because was suffering from obesity and had fallen into depression as a result.

She still weighed less than one hundred twenty pounds and had a BMI of nineteen or less. Upon arrival in the hotel, she had weighed one hundred nineteen pounds. Since she had lost a little weight during her stay, she would probably been in the lower teens by now. But what was this supposed to have to do with the evaluation of whether or not she was fit to work?

It surely needn't be mentioned that she did not appear for her appointment.

But if you imagine that her decision was respected, you would be wrong. After all, when she gave the personnel at the lakeside

Castle her personal information upon check-in, she had also contractually relinquished independent thought and free will. On the evening of the same day as her appointment, a nurse she had never seen before knocked on her door and pertly informed her that she had failed to come at the dictated time to be weighed. She was required to make up for this by coming the next morning at the same time.

"Why?"

Angela asked, and this straightforward question made the nurse start to stutter.

She was completely thrown off balance. She was no longer able to communicate verbally and coherently with Angela. Her grasp of her mother tongue failed her, and she could not articulate her thoughts.

Instead of explaining to Angela what relevance or meaning the measurement of her weight could possibly have, she simply spluttered, "I'm just doing my job. Weighing the patients is something the doctors require of me. I don't need to explain myself to you."

Angela was shocked by the nurse's petulance. She riposted, "If it has to do with me, and you want something from me, but I don't share your opinion, then you most certainly owe me an explanation as to why I should obey this order of yours that seems devoid of all connection to real-world concerns. If you persist in adopting the attitude that you needn't explain the necessity of measuring gravity's pull on my bodily mass, I will persist in ignoring your demands to come be weighed."

This representative of the medical community shot back snippily, "Fine. Then I'll just have to write a memorandum about this incident for your file."

The poor woman was quite undone by Angela standing up to her.

If Angela hadn't been so pissed off, she might have felt sorry for the nurse.

With that, Angela considered the entire unpleasant incident concluded. Be careful when you choose your profession. If I had ordered the nurse to jump off of a one hundred fifty foot bridge, Angela wondered as she closed the door of her temporary housing, would she have complied? She could hear the furious footfalls of the nurse storming toward the elevator.

You can't make shit better by painting it in pastels, she mused to herself.

Angela turned on the television. She happened on the nightly news. It was a visual reminder of how much suffering existed in the world.

Like it or not, this incident, this event heightened Angela's awareness for this sort of mental decrepitude, and she found herself paying attention at breakfast to who was willing to be weighed.

It might be difficult to believe, but almost everyone here was willing to stand in line in the morning and be weighed.

The line reminded her of well-circulated pictures in print and on television of former East Germany. Instead of the scales in front of the door to the nurses' station, signs were hung outside stores in the former German Democratic Republic that read, "Bananas Today".

Angela's unvoiced comment to the other patients' obsequiousness was, Get up! Get up and stand in line!

The final examination

or …
What good had it done Angela?

Angela had finally absolved three weeks at the Castle. In hindsight, the time had passed fairly quickly.

Today she had to go through some of the concluding examinations. To be specific, there was the concluding physical examination, the concluding psychological examination, the concluding individual therapy session, the concluding group therapy session, and last but not least the concluding interview with the physiotherapist.

In the concluding physical examination the doctor and Angela discovered that she had reached none of the goals set for her recovery. Those were improved physical performance, improved concentration, freedom from pain, and a few other desires.

Four of four intentions, or, rather, goals, had unfortunately not been achieved. What great results, Angela thought as she talked over the fantastic outcome of the examination with her therapist.

Still, Angela's doctor and the therapist responsible for her tried their very best and took exceptionally good care of Angela. Her doctor had even prepared tealeaves including lavender extract for her, and had packed them in a small plastic bag for her so she could use them later. The doctor was hoping to help stop Angela from sinking into nightmares while she slept.

Her doctor had even asked Angela to stay in contact with her after being released from Lunatic Castle with a Lakeside View so she could continue to track Angela's progress. This woman poured her heart and soul into helping Angela. Her effort and concern were laudable.

A flood of academics

or …
Nothing but brilliant minds?

Angela found it curious that seemingly only scholars, people in positions of leadership, learned men and woman, knowledge workers, and intellectuals were in attendance at Lunatic Castle with a Lakeside View. If you struck up a conversation with any of the other patients, they all claimed to belong to one of the aforementioned groups. The same thing came out in group therapy.

The cream of the crop was sitting here: sociologists, managers, engineers, business and political economists, and many other forms of intelligentsia not explicitly named here. All were naturally in leadership positions. In the entirety of the Castle, she had yet to find one single salesperson, handyman, office clerk, maid, or anyone else who worked hard and produced tangible results. If you believe that …

Angela hadn't realized before now that the quality of German education had reached its nadir. Angela's intelligence shrank back in horror as a Vestal virgin before marauding Visigoth soldiers while the grammatical barbs ejaculated by these self-styled academics ricocheted in her eardrums.

Angela was privy to parts of a conversation among graduates from institutions of higher learning spanning a few decades. It went something like this: "Who bag this here belong?"

The reply came from another corner of the room: "I".

She wondered what kind of context could have justified such an exchange and what grammatical hecatombs were being performed here at Lunatic Castle with a Lakeside View. Ever heard of prepositions?

These men and women actually passed themselves off as academics, graduates of higher education, recipients of Bachelor's or Master's Degrees. Sure, she thought, sure. Doesn't a single one of you pearls feel the need or even possess the capacity to speak proper German?

The only question remaining if they truly were students of German universities was, in which country, at what auction, or through what online portal service had they acquired their GED?

Man, you shining examples of failed educational policies, do I have to spell it out for you? Here's a quick reference: Complete sentences require a subject, a verb, and an object! Is no one in Lunatic Castle with a Lakeside View master of the German idiom? thought Angela in a moment of great irritation.

The cornucopia of borrowed Anglicisms in the German language isn't much better, but at least almost everyone understands them, even the people here. At least Angela gave them the benefit of the doubt in that question.

People at Lunatic Castle with a Lakeside View lied and invented tales till the cows came home, or, better yet, until Diogenes gave up all hope.

The authors of the many fairytale or fantasy books that proliferate on the shelves of modern bookstores unwittingly provided the blueprints for the yarns told here.

Fortunately for Angela, she did not belong to the uneducated masses. She could speak German just fine.

During her stay in the lakeside Castle, her delicate linguistic sensibility was maltreated more than once.

Nuts

or …
The usual insanity

Angela couldn't help but feel that any contact with the majority of the other patients was necessarily off-kilter.

She only kept in contact with four other patients of the Castle during her residence there: Molly, who had become more than a simple acquaintance in the meantime; Thomas, who sat at the cafeteria table with her; James, who had led her around the Castle after her arrival; and Ina, another member of her topical group.

From time to time, she was pushed to her limit by a situation with another female patient she had met through polite banter and the beginnings of an acquaintanceship, and who turned out to suffer from paranoia.

I can't be so completely wrong about someone, can I? thought Angela. The patient in question, whose name was the dulcet "Amelia", had appeared entirely normal at the outset.

Angela and Amelia were members of the same topical group, and after the second session, Amelia invited Angela out for a cup of coffee. Amelia seemed nice, so Angela l was happy to accept the invitation.

After topical group therapy they got to talking, and Amelia poured out her heart to Angela. Everything she related appeared believable on the surface, and Angela developed strong feelings of sympathy for Amelia as a result.

Until Amelia just happened to bump into her somewhere on the Castle grounds eight or nine times after that, and gradually Angela became suspicious. The first few times Angela had believed their running into each other to be coincidence. After a certain point, though, she couldn't bring herself to believe in so many coincidences.

Time and again she and Amelia crossed paths somewhere on the Castle grounds. Angela came to believe that Amelia lay in wait for her to have yet another chance to talk to her.

This was a counterproductive gardening method to ease the brand new sprout of their acquaintance into a small but healthy plant of friendship. Instead, it gave Angela an uneasy feeling in her stomach every time she stepped out into the corridors, rooms, or halls of the Castle.

A while after that, Angela developed a healthy skepticism towards Amelia a's stories.

Amelia claimed that every doctor and every patient except Angela l herself didn't like her, even rejected her.

She felt that no one understood her.

She even contended she had been given the worst room in the entire Castle, confided that she suspected someone was slipping something into her food, and always verbally abused the head physician in absentia.

Angela had, through a few meetings with the head physician on different occasions, been impressed with him and had judged him competent, friendly, and attentive. The head physician of Lunatic Castle with a Lakeside View was, in her opinion, extraordinarily approachable, empathic, and kind.

As soon as Angela revealed her opinion of the head physician to Amelia. Amelia revised her earlier statements and suddenly also considered him extraordinarily friendly, kind, and empathic.

Amelia's paranoia became increasingly difficult to tolerate, and became more marked. Then it dawned on Angela all of a sudden. In an instantaneous revelation the veil of friendliness, then politeness, and finally simple tolerance was ripped from before her eyes and she was able to see through to the core of Amelia's tortured, evasive personality. This was a personality that had somehow been severely damaged at some unknown way station on life's long journey.

In every subsequent encounter with Amelia, Angela exercised informed caution.

Later, Angela discovered that this psychologically ill woman compliantly ingested gay happy-makers, as was obviously the norm for all psychologically ill people, without incident or grievance with her meals. In a sense, something was being added to Amelia's food everyday at lunch. She had simply repressed the fact that she was the one slipping herself the drugs.

Either she had stopped taking her pills for a while, or she had recently switched medications. These were the only explanations Angela could find for Amelia's disturbing behavior, or, more accurately, the only explanations she could assume for her manic conduct. That didn't make it any easier for Angela, though.

The poor woman lived in her own wacky, mystic world. Everywhere she looked, she saw conspiracies and betrayal against her. Amelia was deathly afraid of going home, which was, of course, a natural and inevitable development. Amelia was utterly convinced that all around where she lived there were only traitors, spies, and other people who wanted to harm her.

The disturbed woman herself asserted that she had no friends where she lived, much less a boyfriend, life partner, or husband. This needy lady lived all alone. She had related this to Angela in one of their many accidental run-ins.

She also purported to have emigrated from the former Yugoslavia and come to Germany some twenty years ago. Implausibly, she spoke excellent German utterly free of an accent.

The zenith of the whole experience was that she herself clearly believed the multitudinous fantastical stories she told Angela. She believed they were her genuine experiences. The stories she spun were definitely real events in her own head. The poor woman visualized all the fables she wove, and thus rewrote and revised the movie of her own life. The whole thing was completely aberrant, surreal, and kind of creepy, but it was also endlessly tragic.

Amelia often invited Angela to her room for a cup of tea or coffee, or to watch television together, or she found some other pretense. Angela steadfastly found some excuse for turning down every invitation, because she found the whole situation spooky and uncanny.

She didn't want to bluntly turn Amelia down, but she also had a bad feeling in the pit of her stomach when she imagined being alone in a room with Amelia, and she never wanted to place herself in that position. She hoped that Amelia would take the hint sooner or later that Angela didn't want to spend time with her.

Instead, Amelia unwittingly found a new way to instill further discomfort into Angela's daily life. After a while, she started following Angela around just to tell her that she thought Angela was the most attractive and best-dressed woman in all of the lakeside Castle. She repeated this three or four times a day. This plagued Angela, but despite steady pleas to desist, Amelia would not stop.

How bizarre! That was Angela's first, and hopefully last, experience with a stalker.

Angela could have reported Amelia's conduct to the clinic staff, but what good would that have done?

Would it have helped this obviously disturbed person to place that additional burden on her shoulders by denouncing her to the authorities? Would it have been better to possibly be the reason Amelia woke up one morning in the bed of a very different establishment for the mentally ill?

Amelia was nuts, batty, messed up, but she was never malignant. Otherworldly, yes. Stressful, yes. Exhausting, yes. Annoying, yes.

Amelia's stalking led Angela to be extremely conservative in her dealings with the other patients. One fanatic was more than enough for the duration of Angela's stay.

She politely declined to take other patients' e-mail addresses or cell phone numbers, and would not reveal her own personal details to anyone.

Angela regreted the way she acted, and that she never gave any of the other patients a chance to get closer to her, but she had to survive in this jungle, this boundless wilderness, too.

Let's see

or …
Was there anything else?

Afternoons in Lunatic Castle with a Lakeside View were nothing short of monotonous. The therapy sessions offered seldom extended past four o'clock in the afternoon. Dinner wasn't until quarter to seven, leaving the intervening time at the discretion of the patients. Since the Castle was situated in a small village, there were precious few diversions available in the vicinity, all of which Angela had exhausted within a couple of days, much to her dismay.

The other patients, excepting a sparse handful, took more than a little getting used to. So Angela spent her afternoons on extended constitutionals, in front of the television, playing mahjongg, or engrossed in some other similar time killer, biding her time until the gorging that took place in the cafeteria every eventide.

Since her time in the lakeside Castle was drawing to a close, she found it ever harder to keep herself occupied.

Evenings were nice. She had a standing telephone appointment with her husband Werner at seven thirty every night. She felt like a teenager at the height of puberty, having a telephone date with the man she was in love with every evening!

And finally, after many weeks, she was finally palpably close to her goal. Her departure was near. Four days from now Angela would exit stage left from the farce, or perhaps tragicomedy, that had been her stay here.

Before her planned departure she had to take another psychological test. This very same test had been administered to her shortly after she had checked in here, and was now to be completed once again at the end of her stay. The purpose of the brace of tests was to monitor her psyche upon entry a few weeks ago and exit, and determine if their had been an improvement in her psychological condition.

Angela was still slightly unnerved by questions about her sexuality or partner, but she had to answer them to complete the test, which was taken on a PC.

Since many of the patients seemed to have trouble answering the test questions, everyone was given a full two hours for the test. Angela breezed through the test at check-in and check-out in less than half an hour.

Interestingly enough, when Angela returned to her room one day just before leaving forever, she found a final questionnaire waiting for her with questions about her impressions of the entire establishment.

There were questions about cleanliness of the room; the politeness of the cleaning personnel, the food service personnel, and all the rest of the personnel; but also about the work of the psychologists and therapists. They could all be graded on a scale from one to five.

Of course the questionnaire was completely anonymous, or at least that's what the introductory text to the questionnaire assured. Uh-huh.

How stupid did the rehabilitation clinic's management think their patients were? Anonymous?

There were questions on the questionnaire for the patient's gender, departure date, arrival date, birthday, and even the building they were housed in.

Very anonymous.

What do you want to bet that many of the Castle's best and brightest dutifully filled out the "anonymous" questionnaire and deposited it in the comments box?

The questionnaire was only intended as an instrument to help improve the Castle's services, of course.

Without a shadow of a doubt. What else could it be for? And how could anyone dream of thinking otherwise?

New construction

or …
The new, much larger fortress of beds

The Castle was to obtain reinforcements. Years ago the construction of a new building had been planned, and now the new building stood on the threshold of completion. The new building was to be ready for habitation two weeks after Angela left.

The magnificent building had earned the scorn of many of the patients, because most of them would be forced to repack their belongings and move into it, even if they had just arrived at the Castle and unpacked a couple of days ago.

Not everyone was affected by the move. The acute patients stayed where they were. Those were the patients who had been committed to the Castle by a doctor, and who were here to heal and be monitored, not to enjoy a typical rehabilitation visit. Only the rehabilitation and spa patients benefitted from the new building and its rooms.

Angela had heard that it didn't matter whether the patients present were scheduled to remain a few more weeks, or scant days. As soon as the new building was finished, all were to move into it.

This was an order from on high.

Angela got her information about the moving of the "old" patients to the new building from her tablemate Thomas.

Thomas had wanted to leave before the move was necessary. Upon the grand opening of the new building, he only had two more days in the lakeside Castle. His individual therapist had unfortunately had to inform Thomas that shortening his scheduled stay was not possible.

The patients of the old Castle and their families, the developer, the builder, and all of the handymen and construction workers involved in the construction were allowed to tour the new building before it opened.

The rooms were really quite beautiful, and seventy to eighty percent of the future rooms for patients would be blessed with a coveted view of the lake. Exactly how many was not yet known at the time of the tour.

Still, in Angela's opinion, the new building had some disadvantages.

There were no televisions or radios in the rooms. The reasoning behind that was to stimulate the sense of community. In the new building it was claimed there were a sufficient number of social rooms and communal television lounges. How, though, were the resident patients to agree on the channel and television show they would all watch when so many different character types and educational levels clashed here?

Or was there perchance another explanation for this choice of furnishings? Could it be that the building had cost much more than estimated, and now other corners had to be cut? Was the clinic administration pinching pennies by striking televisions from the budget?

Maybe this was nothing but pure speculation. Who knew the real answer? She didn't.

This same cost cutting was to be felt later in the room cleaning service. The patients who would be future residents of the new building would be cleaning their own rooms. The cleaning personnel responsible for Angela's room had let her know about this development.

The armies of cleaning ladies would only be permitted to clean the common rooms. Some of the cleaning dragons employed here would surely be relieved of duty.

She wondered if the developer had thought through the planning and realization of the grounds around the new building. That is, if he knew what the consequences would be of cementing double width wooden chaise lounges into the garden. This kind of garden planning would doubtless be an open invitation to many of the patients to let themselves be lulled into slothfulness Angela reflected during her tour around the grounds of the new building.

There would also be testers galore among the patients in heat to verify the robust construction of the chaise lounges, for they were perfectly constructed for getting to know the opposite or the same sex more intimately. On many a night there would be plenty of squeaking boards to be heard. Angela certainly didn't relish the thought of being one of the twenty to thirty percent of the patients who roomed on the garden side of the building. The developer had failed to take the necessity of a good night's sleep into account when the garden was designed.

Even the doctors and therapists were uneasy about the new structure. At this point in time, Angela didn't want to be a guest at Lunatic Castle with a Lakeside View in Bad Kleeblatt again any time soon, if ever, anyway.

She hoped that the effects of the rehabilitation would take full effect once she was home again.

She was content to forego moving into the new building she and her husband Werner had toured, because her hotel room was markedly more comfortable and personal than what she had seen.

The taming of the shrew

or …
Just when you thought it couldn't get worse …

Angela had always held the opinion that no one was truly ugly.

Beauty, or so her personal philosophy went, was truly solely to be found in the eyes of the beholder. Any ugly duckling could turn into a beautiful swan, or, more precisely, in every ugly duckling there was a beautiful swan waiting to emerge.

But then in every beautiful swan there also lurked an ugly duckling.

There was always something attractive about aesthetically disadvantaged people. Perhaps it was their Pollyanna personality, their sunny smile, unblemished skin, or sparkling eyes. Angela and lived and grown under the credo that every human is born to bring light into this world in their own way, and that this light always makes itself manifest, as long as you knew how to look for it.

Then she met a woman who, for the first time, would cause a crisis in belief in Angela's soul. Angela found the limit of her philosophy in Lunatic Castle with a Lakeside View.

Among Angela's peers at the Castle was a woman who weighed an estimated four hundred pounds, perhaps more. This woman had an inflated self-assurance to match her physical dimensions; it came across as sickeningly bloated. That royal self-assurance was what the woman attributed her behavior to.

This in all dimensions corporeal and social plus-sized dame conducted herself as a diva might. She verbally lashed every female Castle employee, and should none be handy, she abused a female patient instead.

This gaudily dressed woman among women took up fully two adjacent chairs without armrests when she sat. The first time Angela saw her, two different images of large things dangerous for all of humanity flashed through her head: the hole in the ozone layer, and the Stay Puft Marshmallow Man.

This fleshy woman sat at the same table as Angela in one of the ergotherapy sessions. The Rotund One wanted to sew dolls' clothes, which by itself is just fine.

The theatrics started when one of the therapists approached the fleshy woman and asked her if she needed any help cutting the dolls' clothes. The sweet-tempered, well-intentioned therapist shouldn't have asked that.

The hellhound began to bark; the squall broke over the defenseless therapist. She didn't stop ranting for the next three quarters of an hour. "Who told you I wanted your help?

How did the thought even occur to you to ask me if I need assistance?

Do I look helpless?

You have no idea what I've achieved in my life!

What I've learned!

How many dolls' dresses I've already sewn!

For all you know, I'm an accomplished seamstress! Or even just a hobby seamstress!"

That's all true, but who cares, Angela thought while trying to imagine herself in a place devoid of strident noises.

But the hellhound had been awoken. She rattled her chains.

The fat fury had been roused from her restless slumber. This flabby woman would not stop raving.

The tsunami of jumbled words, curses, and epithets that swept over the therapist was too much for her. The therapist left the room of terror, the lair of the hellhound, the can of hairspray that had been left out in the noontime midsummer sun too long, under a paper-thin pretext.

When Angela was confronted with this woman and her behavior, she associated her with a *toro* in the arena of a bullfight. The bull snorted and pawed at the ground with his hooves. Swords stuck out of the back of his neck. Finally, the powerful, furious animal charged.

This vision of Eve driven from paradise was unbelievable!

Different day, same woman. Angela and the Fat One had to work together on a presentation in a topical group. The room in which this took place was smallish. Somewhere between ten and fifteen people could fit in it.

Now the hellhound had a real problem. All of the chairs in the room had armrests.

This time it was a female work-study student who wanted to show her some kindness and polite treatment, and thus offered to scare up two chairs without armrests, so she could sit and would not be forced to stand for the duration of the presentation. The ensuing explosion of words nearly blasted the student out of the room.

The fat woman seemed to be competing with Wotan, only instead of covering Freia with gold, she tried to cover the student so completely with words, raven black and venomous, that not a ray of light could penetrate.

"Who the hell do you think you are? And what do you think I am, an invalid? As if I couldn't sit on one of the seats here!"

The obese hellhound plopped down in one of the chairs. The poor chair, Angela cringed inwardly. If objects could scream in pain ...

All of the other patients in the room stared at the chair and braced themselves for the worst. It groaned under the enormous weight it was now forced to support. The chair legs bent wide, but the chair did not buckle. Who would have guessed?

The heavy woman was still left with a problem to solve, though. She was stuck.

Man, how Angela enjoyed that moment!

How the fat woman eventually managed to liberate herself from the chair that was taking its revenge, Angela did not know, and she wasn't able to find out later.

She didn't want to witness the comedy of the emancipation from the chair and the accompanying verbal *auto de fe* that followed. She heard reports that the woman let loose with extremely loud tirades that eventually lighted upon every person in the room while she was being freed from the overly vindictive furniture.

But as soon as a man entered the room, this fury, this hellhound, this fat diva morphed into Circe.

She started flirting for all she was worth with everything she had to offer. She was suddenly truly nice, even charming. She could laugh. It was unbelievable.

Angela found the situation absolutely surreal. Once again the feeling crept up on her that she was stuck in *Alice in Wonderland.*

When this woman spoke, it was like bolts of lightning hitting cottages of wood and thatched roofs. Her conviction of her own rightness was so complete that she had a standing scorched earth policy concerning everyone else and their opinions.

Man, thought Angela, life not only takes place every day, it's also full of surprises.

Saving the best for last

or …
The wellness oasis in the tower

Up until now, Angela hasn't mentioned the best part of her stay at the castle. That was without a doubt physiotherapy!

The physiotherapy sessions were held in what was called the tower. Here in the rooms of the tower some thirty therapists bustled about, always engaged in trying to make their patients' stays just that much more pleasant.

Lady Luck smiled on Angela, and she was assigned to a very nice young physiotherapist. That doesn't mean that the rest of the physiotherapists weren't nice, but this one was exceptionally nice!

She was a wellspring of light in Angela's existence at Lunatic Castle with a Lakeside View. Angela received foot massages, Lymphatic Drainage Therapy, back massages, and, not to be forgotten, the hydrojet. The latter was about the same size as a small waterbed and used water nozzles to massage the patient.

The hydrojet was awesome. The fifteen minutes allotted for each use were definitely too short. Half a day would have been a much better place to start for time spent on this miracle machine.

Angela's physiotherapist also secured a very labor intensive and expensive form of support for her to help with her foot drop. This therapist had pulled all the strings she could to get approval for the construction of a carbon ankle-foot orthosis (AFO) for Angela. Without this AFO, Angela had great difficulty lifting her right foot.

Angela made a mental note to thank the very kind physiotherapist profusely one last time for her tremendous support.

Angela s final days in the House of Loose Screw Heads in Bad Kleeblatt

or …
The light at the end of the tunnel

The sun rose on Angela's last days at the lakeside Castle. She wanted to be a part of the final group therapy sessions available to her. She didn't want to forego that pleasure.

In her thoughts, though, she was already gone.

The remaining days consisted of physical therapy, which Angela called improved yoga, for Angela was not fond of yoga; and further therapeutic measures she wished to end her stay with.

The day before she had been intentionally passive during the group terror session. She discovered that day that this was the only way she could be a part of the topical group discussions without nursing a grudge.

Even if the therapist did not condone this. He made that crystal clear to Angela. To put it mildly, Angela couldn't care less what the therapist bleated at her; Monday was just around the corner!

Hello Sunday!
Angela just couldn't wait for the coming Monday!

What a beautiful day at Lunatic Castle with a Lakeside View in Bad Kleeblatt, Angela saluted the rising sun in her thoughts as it woke her. Her penultimate day had begun.

The morning got off to a good start. After she had arisen from bed, she slipped out on her luxurious balcony and felt calm seep deep into her mind as she watched the sun rise over the lake. In the background, the radio that was integrated into her television played dreamy, reflective music. It was a perfect morning.

She was in top form and determined not to let anything or anyone ruin her good mood.

In contrast to the solitude she had decided upon the night before, her last daily schedule was a full one. You go, girl! Angela congratulated herself.

Breakfast tasted better this morning than it ever had. Why was that? Where did her good mood come from?

Even the insane hecticness around her in the large breakfast room, the swarm around the buffets, glanced off of her good mood on this last day before her departure.

She ate her last breakfast in the lakeside Castle. Today all of the other patients looked different to her, as if she were viewing them through rose-colored glasses. Had she perhaps already become too mild in her not so old age?

During cardiovascular training on the stationary bicycle today, she had the privilege of sitting across from a shirtless man who was at least seventy-five years old. There was a haunted house situated near her home in the state of Schleswig-Holstein that was seasonally open to the paying public every year. The ghosts one could see in this haunted house were no more horrifying than the sight of this man.

Angela had planned one more hour of physical therapy in the afternoon, exercise for the decrepit, as she liked to call it, and an hour of fitness for the healthy as a treat to herself. That rounded out her day of activities.

Back in her room and looking out the picture window at that view she couldn't get enough of, she registered that she was hungry enough to eat a horse. Let the battle of the dinner buffet begin! she thought.

The people sitting around her at the table all claimed they were sad to see her go.

Angela wasn't so sure. Maybe they were just being polite. Would they really have been happy if Angela had accepted a two week extension to her stay, or even longer? The therapists and doctors had suggested no less than a four week extension for her. That was one question that would remain unanswered. Anything Angela could say would be unadulterated speculation.

Monday. The day of her departure from Lunatic Castle with a Lakeside View had dawned, much to Angela's joy.

On this day, she had risen around five in the morning and packed her four suitcases. She finished packing around seven and began straightening up the room.

After that job was done, Angela showered and washed her hair.

Grooming being dispensed with, and after looking in the mirror to her satisfaction, it was time to part from her home of the last four weeks and head to the reception hall with all of her luggage in tow.

But first there was the waiting for the elevator that felt like it would never come.

She sat on her bulging suitcases and waited for her darling, her husband Werner. But not everyone chose to understand that. They advanced on her with broad smiles of greeting, the understanders of women and their compatriots, the collected male potential energy of the Castle.

And what did they actually ask Angela?

"Are you leaving?"

She thought, no, no, I simply like sitting on suitcases in reception halls. Call it a hobby. She secretly asked herself if they really meant this question. But she only said:

"Yes, I'm waiting for my husband to pick me up and take me home."

Words cannot describe how delighted she was to be allowed to return to her old, complacent, entirely normal life!

Hooray! Hooray! Dear, familiar home, I'm on my way!

Angela's résumé

or ...
Looking back

Angela's adventure can be summed up as follows: the male patients of the Castle had majored in fast hands at the Academy of Broads. Too bad for them there were no more slots free in the classes for men with slow hands, so they persevered in what was available to them and received a Master's Degree in fast hands. For this accomplishment they deserve belated congratulations!

Optical and communicative overkill was par for the course in the lakeside Castle, as well. All of the midday talk shows, whatever they were called, could pack their bags and go home. Here in Lunatic Castle with a Lakeside View every eccentricity imaginable was available to the voyeuristic entertainment industry for the amusement of the folks at home.

Dear casting teams, you can have your pick of the best here! All of your future reality shows could be invested with a spark of novelty and life at the Castle. Your casting couches would never again be empty.

Angela was never quite sure why the patients here were always so willing to make a bigger problem out of two small ones.

There were plenty of patients in Lunatic Castle with a Lakeside View ...or, how Molly said, – The House of Loose Screw Heads – who suffered from psychosomatic illnesses. How could the patients be expected to adjust to each other?

Intelligence and understanding separate homo sapiens from the other mammals. Why for all the world was this evolutionary advantage traded for animal passions for the duration of a short stay in Bad Kleeblatt?

This applies to men and women in equal measure, of course. No one in the lakeside Castle was forced into sex. It was all consummated consensually. Why were intelligence and responsibility collectively repressed?

Angela couldn't understand it then, and she still can't now.

But everyone in the Castle had reached the age of majority. Every single patient checked in here was responsible for themselves. In the end, every person must take responsibility for his or her own life and actions. Angela didn't want to anoint herself the upholder of moral standards, and she certainly didn't want to play judge and jury over the other patients. It was not her right to do that.

Everyone makes their own happiness, of course. Everyone had to decide for themselves how far they went, what they allowed, and where they drew the line. Still, it took no seer to predict the strife that followed on the heels of these choices.

She went through life in a different gear. She was in the "I know what I have, but don't know what I would be getting" gear, the "I'm happy with my choice of partner" gear.

The doctors and therapists performed their duties well, and frequently cut to the quick of their patients' illusions and baseless fears. Despite that, after having enjoyed the hospitality of the employees of Lunatic Castle with a Lakeside View in Bad Kleeblatt for a few weeks, she did not feel compelled to return to this space any time in the foreseeable future. If, though, it once again became necessary, she would not hesitate once again to impose on the hospitality of the Castle staff. Yes, she would check-in here again if there was no other option, but only to benefit from the help offered by the therapists and doctors. All of the other accessories to this central purpose were superfluous.

Angela and Molly sat on the balcony outside Angela's hotel room on Angela's last evening there. They met in Angela's room because Molly's wasn't half as luxurious, and they were on the balcony because Angela's room was for non-smokers. There was a smoke detector hanging from the ceiling that Angela wasn't interested in testing.

Molly avowed that she was not addicted. Smoking just calmed her nerves, and was a kind of therapy for her. Besides that, a cigarette tasted so good after such a harried day, and tasted even better in agreeable company, of course. So the two of them soaked in the view of the setting sun over the lake one last time together.

"Hey," Molly began, "looking back, do you think your stay here was good for you?"

Angela considered a while, then replied, "Yes, I think it did much more for me than I could have imagined beforehand with all of the prejudices I brought with me. Sure, there were scads of men and women, birds of paradise, testosterone bombs, and estrogen pumps, who made our lives in this clinic difficult at every turn. Most days, I found the other patients' pretentiousness grating. I have to admit, many times I wished I weren't subjected to the theatrics, the self-dramatizations and the public shows so abundant here. But I am thankful for the direction and possibilities the therapists showed us, thankful for them shining a light into the fog surrounding me."

Angela had contacted a behavioral therapist near her home four days previous.

"You know something, Molly?"

Angela continued.

"A while ago I came to understand that there's no shame in checking in to a psychosomatic clinic. Group and individual therapy, as well as the colorful characters I already mentioned, were very helpful to me in accepting my own problems and even recognizing what my problems are. A few days ago I called a therapist not far from where we live, and I have an appointment with him two weeks after I get home.

"In the future, I'm not going to pretend to be strong anymore. I will accept my weaknesses and admit them to myself. Accept that I have weaknesses, that I'm allowed to have weaknesses, and that they are a part of me. I don't always have to be strong anymore."

"Yeah," Molly said, "I feel the same way.

I requested a list of therapists close to my home, too, and I'm going to call them all tomorrow.

I'm hoping that I'll be given an appointment with an adequate therapist in the near future, just like you were."

Molly looked out over the lake, lost in her own thoughts.

The definition of happiness

or …
Inner contentment

What does happiness really mean?

Happiness is an emotional state, and as such is experienced and defined differently by every person.

For some, happiness is circumscribed by money. For others, it is related to feeling and receiving human warmth. Still others consider happiness nothing more than the freedom to be master of one's own life. I, Angela, share this latter philosophy.

Whatever your own, personal vision of happiness is, I hope that vision becomes reality for you.

Conclusion

Based on her own adventure in the psychosomatic clinic in Bad Kleeblatt, Angela can only recommend to everyone who has also had this experience, or who soon will, to let it be known. Much to her own surprise, she found the courage to answer truthfully when the employees or members of her fitness club, her friends, her acquaintances, or her extended family members asked her why she had been away so long. She told them that her fears and the trauma she had experienced led her to check in to a psychosomatic clinic.

Her best advice to every psychologically ill human is not to keep the fears bottled up inside. Angela would plead with every affected person to raze the imaginary walls of fear, the barricades of inner petrification, and not to give the fear an inch of ground.

The decisive point is that an afflicted person lets go of the victim role and takes charge of his own fate, no matter what happened to him in the past. Even if that is easier said than done, it is of the utmost importance.

Once a person had accepted and analyzed his clinical picture for himself, he will be able to see that he should switch gears into neutral for a while in order to process the past, arrive in the present, then switch gears back into drive to welcome the future.

He will once again be able to see that life is truly worth living, and that there is always a light at the end of every tunnel.

If a person makes their troubles known, they will receive support from people they wouldn't have guessed.

If one decides to occupy a room in a rehabilitation clinic for a while, it is up to him whether he takes on the role of player in the game, or whether he would rather sit in the stands and watch the game from afar. There is much less danger of injury in the stands.

There are more colors than just black and white! The world and all of life exists in a chromatic palette!

Murphy's Law is hypothetical!

Once those who think the world is bad, and that everything that can go wrong will go wrong finally accept that they are the designers of their own happiness, Murphy's Law will lose its power over their lives.

The journey is the reward.

There is no shame in seeking help in a psychosomatic clinic. It can be the beginning of a new path to a life free of the burdens of the past.

If a visit to a rehabilitation clinic doesn't feel right, if the inner barriers are too high, one can and should still seek the assistance of a professional therapist. Your doctor of confidence can provide you with a list. Angela.

More about me, Angela …

Why in the name of all that's holy must I check in to Lunatic Castle with a Lakeside View by the cold light of day?

Perhaps I should introduce myself first:

My name is Angela. I am, as those versed in matters Teutonic can easily recognize, female. I'm five feet five inches and one hundred eighteen pounds. Yours truly was born in 1971 – in the lovely month of May in a suburb of Wuppertal. I'm naturally dark-haired, a quality I have thus far retained, I have green eyes, and I'm happily married. I have two sons who are, naturally, well raised, dreams come true for any parent and future parent-in-law.

On top of that, I am the proud owner of a huge aquarium, a crazy dog and a free-roaming Greek tortoise.

I live with my small family in a backwoods town in the German state of Schleswig-Holstein, and before yours truly became sick I enjoyed a good standing in my career.

My fellow humans claim to find me fairly attractive, but this is, as always in life, in the eye of the beholder. Some people, such as my husband Tyler quite simply wear blinders. Then again, there are a few days a year when I can live with my looks just fine.

Two and a half years ago I was the victim of medical malpractice, and since then suffer from acute insomnia, various phobias, and intense trauma.

Much to my regret, I had no choice but to undergo eleven operations in the two and a half years previous, of those seven in quick succession. The further operations were necessary to save my life and prevent further damage to my right leg after the first two planned operations, one of which went well, but the second of which failed and nearly killed me.

Despite the speedy assistance from the doctors who treated me after the malpractice I am still left with permanent damage: among other things an eight and a half inch scar running from my knee down my leg. As a result of the malpractice

I have lasting visible and invisible damage to my now perpetually sick leg.

Thus have I dug deep into life's reserve of luck. Such a pity, for now I will have very little chance at a career as a model for pantyhose, ignoring for the moment my exorbitantly high age for a model.

The caring, deeply concerned processing clerk responsible for me at my health insurer sent me a written invitation to a full body examination due to my illness. If I would be so kind, I should please present myself at a rehabilitation clinic, which I will call "Lunatic Castle with a Lakeside View", in Bad Kleeblatt for a thorough examination, and if my busy schedule allowed it, I would be more than welcome to check in for a few weeks. The therapists and doctors working at Lunatic Castle with a Lakeside View would decide about my return to working life during my protracted stay there.

I had and still have great difficulty accepting my new situation in life as well as reintegrating into what now seems to me to be a new world, so despite my inhibitions concerning this not entirely optional invitation, I should say in all fairness that

I hoped my stay in the House of Loose Screw Heads would help me get things in focus. I considered it a good outlet for processing and making my peace with the previous events.

Before I continue, I would like to mention that my husband Tyler and my children Henry and Logan staunchly stood by me, caught me, and in the end re-imbued me with my lost will to live during the difficult times after the failed operation and the many ensuing operations and my accompanying ill health, during the mood swings, during the constant, repeated ups and downs.

Many, many thanks to the three of you!

When the time came to part with my family and my familiar surroundings on the Tuesday I was to leave, the day of my departure into the unknown, it was not without grave concerns in my mind.

I had many reservations about this rehabilitation or spa, call it what you will, from the very beginning.

Many times my prejudices were confirmed or even deepened; it was so bad that, besides my family, I only told my best friend which rehabilitation clinic I would be staying in during the coming weeks.

I assumed others would incorrectly assess the situation and suddenly consider me simple, imbecilic, or deviant.

I wanted to avoid that at all costs.

So I repeated to myself during my stay at Lunatic Castle with a Lakeside View: I'm here now, and I'm going to finish what I've started.

My mantra was and remains „everything will turn out well". I believed and still believe in self-fulfilling prophecies.

After a few weeks as a guest at Lunatic Castle with a Lakeside View I realized that one truly could receive help here at the Castle as long as one was willing to open oneself to the therapy and therapists. At least that's my hard-won wisdom from my rehabilitation.

The therapists were genuinely concerned about their patients' health and tried to pick up on and work through their mostly imagined and occasionally real problems with them. Of course they couldn't fix the problems or take them away from the patients, but still, one was headed in the right direction, was on the right path. It felt right and good to see how the land lies and to be handed a *Marshall plan* for support.

Things take time. Grass doesn't grow faster if you pull on it.

Acknowledgements

I want to thank everyone who helped me in word and deed to finish this undertaking. Specifically:

My husband Werner, who left me alone while I was writing, and who supported me and motivated me to write this book.

My son Tobias, who gave me a few tips.

My son Torben, who gave me tips and supported me as he was able.

And last but not least: My translator, Andrew Rucker Jones.

Many heartfelt thanks for everything!

About the Author

I, Bärbel Kiy, was born in a small general hospital in Schwelm on Saturday, the 27th of May 1961, the only daughter of the professional mechanical engineer Horst Schmidt and his wife Erika.

I have been married to the love of my youth for the past three decades. We have had two sons together.

Before I was torn out of the regular flow of life by a debilitating sickness, I was a procurement manager, branch office manager, and personnel officer for a temporary agency.

My illness has forced me to completely rearrange my life. That's how I discovered writing as a form of therapy.

I now dedicate myself to exploring burning social issues, and shine a light into the shadowy corners of existence that have long slumbered. I wish to drag these sable taboos and fears out into daylight to be examined for what they are, and named without shame or trepidation.

I live with my family in a mid-sized town near the capital of the German state of Schleswig-Holstein.

Visit me on my homepage: **www.baerbel-kiy.de**